ENTERTAINING AT HOME

ENTERTAINING AT HOME

INSPIRATIONS FROM CELEBRATED HOSTS

RONDA CARMAN
FOREWORD BY INDIA HICKS
PRINCIPAL PHOTOGRAPHY BY
MATTHEW MEAD AND MICHAEL HUNTER

Rizzoli
NEW YORK

New York · Paris · London · Milan

FOREWORD
India Hicks

"Claire, how much do you like it when I suddenly say there aren't going to be twenty-five people for dinner, but rather fifty?" I ask Top Banana in our kitchen as she rolls out pastry for hors d'oeuvres. "Are you cross?" I ask. "No, I know you too well," she replies, smiling patiently.

I always look forward to having friends and family join us. I have fun setting the table in various ways, changing locations, and thinking up new decorations, whether it is a table sprinkled with lucky nuts we have collected from the beach, or Eiffel Tower–sized vases with palm fronds, or a simple assortment of shells mixed with votive candles. I often change the tablecloth from formal white to a stretch of colored linen fabric left over from reupholstering bedroom chairs, or possibly an Indian-mirrored bedspread. Depending on my mood, I like to mix up the location, decorations, and the guests as much as David, my other half, likes to mix up the drinks.

I love to host parties. I also appreciate being a guest at someone else's simple supper. Or lively lunch. Or revolutionized black tie. Thank God, then, for Ronda Carman's gorgeous new book. It's an invitation to the imaginative parties given in the enchanting houses of celebrated hosts. Ronda takes us on a tour of homes to learn the ins and outs of entertaining from her friends and favorite tastemakers who have blazed trails in interior design, culinary arts, and fashion.

Anyone who likes to entertain at home will delight in all of the lovely bits and the behind-the-scenes planning, like finding the best goodies at the farmer's market and stocking the larder so that you don't find yourself missing a crucial ingredient when it comes time to put the dishes on that carefully planned menu into the oven. We learn the secrets to how these spirited individuals make everything look effortless. And once learned, those skills only get sharper, and then you are free to focus on the fun—like tying up flowers or lanterns or balloons with miles of fishing line.

In case you don't have five children who can be enlisted to compile playlists, or houseguests who can be convinced to put their genius flower arranging skills to good use, there are tips for doing those things too.

I now fully intend to nick all of the good ideas seen throughout this lovely book and will also angle for an invitation to any lunch, dinner, or Fat Tuesday from these celebrated hosts.

Of course the door is always open for them here as well. I will just wait a minute or two before letting Top Banana know that we are expecting a few more for dinner.

INTRODUCTION

Ronda Carman

As a child, while most of my friends played with dolls pretending to be mothers or school-teachers, I hosted imaginary dinner parties in my parents' dining room. Apple juice with a touch of Sprite became Champagne, while chopped black olives served in crystal bowls doubled as caviar. If I was feeling particularly extravagant, I would layer Cool Whip over Jell-O in shallow wine glasses. Being alone in the sunlit room, admiring my creations and staring at a china closet full of treasures, filled me with a sense of pride and endless possibilities.

I especially loved holiday meals. For Thanksgiving, I would always insist that my family members wear their "fancy" clothes for dinner—my younger sisters rolled their eyes. And at Christmastime, I was all about red velvet dresses for the girls—Pappagallo, Laura Ashley, Jessica McClintock—and if a dress had a large lace collar, so much the better.

I was fortunate to grow up in a household that loved hosting family and friends. From baby showers and movie nights to Sunday lunches with the preacher, my mom and dad would invite everyone and anyone into our home. Their celebrations were never pretentious, and they always adopted the-more-the-merrier philosophy. An extra plate could easily be added to any table.

In my early twenties, I met my mentor, Elizabeth Shouse. Walking into her home for the first time was otherworldly. I had never witnessed such beauty or opulence, not to mention her spectacular collection of china, silver, and crystal. A massive antique Baccarat chandelier, suspended high above the mahogany table, cast color around the room. Deep pink, raw silk drapes mirrored the color of Mottahedeh Tobacco Leaf plates on display in the china cabinet and pale pink hand-blown stemware. I quickly went from babysitter to Elizabeth's girl Friday. From polishing silver and peeling shrimp to setting the table and pouring wine, I loved it all.

It was also during this time that I learned to cook. Each weekend I would go to the library and check out every Junior League cookbook I could get me hands on. I worked my way through them, eventually graduating to cookbooks by Lee Bailey and Chuck Williams. However, while there was an abundance of cookbooks, entertaining books were lacking. The few that did exist became regular reading. I would photocopy every page and create large binders filled with notes.

Around the same period, I discovered *Bon Appétit* and became obsessed with the magazine's "Entertaining with Style" feature, produced by Bettie Bearden Pardee. I savored every word and clipped my favorite columns. Recently I came across a notebook filled with my handwritten notes and an outline for an entertaining book. Even though a dream, at twenty-one years old, I could have scarcely imagined that one day I would write my own tome.

Throughout the years I have been lucky to glean wisdom and inspiration from many talented people. However, this is not meant to be a volume on how to entertain properly, but rather a glimpse of real people at home nurturing friends and family. It is my hope that it is as much aspirational as it is inspirational.

RISE AND SHINE

A GATHERING IN THE GREENHOUSE
Jay Draper and Mark Thompson

Perched atop a small hill in Birmingham, Alabama, sits Shoppe, a beloved plant and flower emporium housed in a Victorian-style greenhouse and a 1920s bungalow. The store is just across the street from the home of purveyors Jay Draper and Mark Thompson. While many would shun the idea of working in such close proximity, the two relish the concept of intermingling work life and family life.

Each day Jay, Mark, and their adorable dog, Cedar, cross the lane and begin their morning work. From the two men shuffling around terra-cotta pots and offering warm greetings at the front door to the aroma of softly scented candles, everything exudes an old-fashioned, neighborly charm. Each detail is purposeful, making customers and guests feel as if they are old acquaintances. The handcrafted, hunter green English conservatory, adjacent to the quaint abode, is a favorite spot for scouting herbs, shrubbery, and unique garden gifts. Today, however, it is a place to gather for a celebratory birthday brunch.

A warm sun-drenched Sunday makes for a picture-perfect afternoon. The hosts welcome each arrival with a glass of pale yellow Alsace gewürztraminer. The complex wine with its peppery apricot aromas is an impeccable pairing for the main dish—lemon-infused Israeli couscous with arugula and crumbled bacon. Both men grew up gardening, farming, and entertaining. Unsurprisingly, fresh and locally sourced food always finds its way onto the menu.

In addition to their green thumbs, Mark and Jay are history buffs and love to collect everything from vintage plates and mismatched water goblets to random pieces of Depression glass. Friends and family have added to their collections. Sentimentality and nostalgia drive their sense of style and design direction. The cumulative look is masculine, feminine, and soulful.

For a lighthearted touch, food is served on Franciscan Ivy plates. First introduced in 1948, the cream and green iconic plates were a fixture on the television sitcoms *I Love Lucy* and *The Donna Reed Show*. Glass cloches filled with yellow ranunculus, suspended from the rafters, create a whimsical ambience. An assortment of wooden tables causally pushed together form a seating area for twenty. To unify the tabletops, Mark uses a cheerful muted-green fabric adorned with daisies. The discount textile was purchased, sewn, and edged just for the occasion. Simple vases, some with marigolds that are grown nearby and others with white daisies, are scattered about the surface. The guests' names are handwritten on charming paper place cards that mimic plates.

After a leisurely brunch, guests linger a little longer for a cup of tea. Candied and spiced pecans, served in their grandmothers' candy dishes, indulge all of those with a sweet tooth. One by one people depart, walking home as the sun commences to set on a memorable day in the neighborhood.

KEEPING
FLOWERS FRESH

Maintaining flowers is easier than you think. Mark and Jay share a few tricks of the trade for keeping beautiful blossoms living longer.

Cut stems on the diagonal. It will increase the surface area and allow the blossoms to take in more water.

Remove any leaves that will be submerged in water once in the vase. Wet leaves will quickly rot.

Mix 2 tablespoons apple cider vinegar with 2 tablespoons granulated white sugar in the vase before adding water and arranging the flowers. The sugar will act as food, while the vinegar will fight bacteria in the water.

To keep flowers tight and fresh, always place them in cold water. Conversely, if you have unopened flowers that you need to speed along, use warm water to force the blooms to open more quickly.

Change the water every few days to avoid growth of bacteria. When changing the water, recut the stems.

BRAISED CARROTS

Serves 8

Braising is not just for meat. Slowly simmering food in liquid is an easy way to create tenderness and flavor. This gentle cooking method can be used for a variety of vegetables.

2 pounds small carrots with tops, peeled
4 tablespoons unsalted butter
1 tablespoon fresh thyme leaves, minced
Juice of 1 orange
½ cup cold water
Salt and black pepper to taste

Trim the tops off the carrots, leaving about 1/2 inch of the green stems attached.

Heat the butter in a large sauté pan over medium-high heat. Add the carrots and cook, stirring from time to time, until tender, 8 to 10 minutes. Add the thyme and stir for an additional 2 minutes. Mix in the orange juice and water and season with salt and pepper. Cover, reduce the heat to low, and let the carrots simmer until nearly all liquid has cooked off, about 10 minutes. Season the carrots with more salt and pepper if needed. Serve warm.

LEMON-INFUSED ISRAELI COUSCOUS WITH BACON AND ARUGULA

Serves 8

While Southerners love to serve up a side of steaming hot grits, Mark and Jay opt for Israeli couscous, sometimes labeled as pearl couscous. The hearty, white, structural pasta holds it shape and pairs wonderfully with a multitude of flavors. It is quick and easy to prepare.

2 tablespoons unsalted butter
1 shallot, finely diced
1 clove minced garlic
Zest of 1 small lemon, minced
2 cups Israeli couscous
2 ½ cups chicken or vegetable stock
Sea salt and cracked black pepper to taste
4 cups baby arugula
2 tablespoons extra-virgin olive oil
8 slices bacon, rendered crisp and crumbled
8 soft-boiled eggs, halved

In a large saucepan heat the butter over a medium-low heat. Add the shallot, garlic, and lemon zest. Sauté for 3 minutes. Be careful not to burn the garlic.

Add the couscous to the saucepan. Briskly stir, ensuring the couscous is evenly coated with the butter mixture. Continue stirring until the couscous is lightly toasted, about 2 minutes.

Add the stock and season with salt and pepper. Bring to a high simmer, then reduce the heat to low. Cover and cook, until the water is absorbed, about 10 minutes.

Meanwhile, vigorously toss the arugula with olive oil in a large Ziploc bag. Then divide the arugula among eight plates.

Remove the couscous from the heat and keep covered. Let stand for 3 minutes. Remove the lid and gently fluff the couscous with a fork. Top each plate of greens with couscous and bacon. Serve eggs alongside the couscous.

A LATE LAZY BREAKFAST
Debbie Propst

While some people prefer eating in more formal spaces, Debbie Propst and her family gather in their breakfast nook for most meals. Nestled within a large kitchen and in close proximity to the butler's pantry, it is a space that is both casual and sophisticated. It is also a favorite spot to assemble friends for a late breakfast on the weekends.

"The kitchen is where I am most comfortable," Debbie admits, "and there is nothing I adore more than being surrounded by people I love." Comfort is precisely what she found in her 1950s Cape Cod saltbox designed by Royal Barry Wills, a master of Cape Cod architecture and a noted author. And although Debbie was not specifically looking for a farmhouse property at the time, she felt at home the moment she stepped inside the Connecticut dwelling. Great bones, an abundance of character, and spacious rooms won her over.

President of One Kings Lane, Debbie turned to the company's in-house interior designer to devise a living plan that would accommodate two children, a dog, and spaces for entertaining. Born in Scotland, Debbie spent her childhood in Spain and the United Kingdom. Southern England fostered her adoration for the farm lifestyle.

Time spent abroad also shaped her cooking philosophy. In keeping with a European sensibility, the hostess often opts for boards of cheeses, fruit, pastries, nuts, prosciutto, eggs, a seasonal signature cocktail, and plenty of coffee and tea. For the first breakfast of autumn, she gathers a group of like-minded neighbors who have not yet met one another.

An abundance of seasonal blooms, including orange dahlias, hellebores, and starflower pincushions, are slipped into a vintage green ceramic vase, while large leafy branches provide a lush and layered atmosphere. An assortment of gourds in a variety of shapes and colors adds an autumnal hue to the house. Little pumpkins also double as place-card holders. "I'm a big fan of place cards, especially when I have guests over who have never met."

Debbie entices everyone into the kitchen for apple cider mimosas while she puts the finishing touches on a rustic pear tart. As the kitchen is the place where everyone ends up eventually, the hostess is perfectly okay with having people around while she is doing some prep work. "I think it is important not to take entertaining too seriously. You want people to feel relaxed and smile when they walk into your home."

DEBBIE'S TABLETOP CHEAT SHEET

For this fall breakfast, Debbie uses a mix of vintage pieces and new tabletop accessories. Here are her favorite resources.

BRASS CANDLEHOLDERS: *vintage Ystad lily design*

CANDLES: *black tapers by Creative Candle*

CHAMPAGNE FLUTES: *vintage*

COFFEE CUPS: *modern ceramic black by Canvas Home*

COPPER LUSTERWARE BOWL: *vintage*

FLATWARE: *Sabre and ivory stainless steel*

NAPKINS: *Harmony*

PITCHER: *Ralph Lauren Home*

PLATES: *Silo classic dinner plates by Farmhouse Pottery*

PLACEMATS: *woven chargers by Juliska*

PLACE CARDS: *small gourds with handwritten name tags*

TABLE RUNNER: *vintage embroidered linen*

TEAPOT: *Tom Dixon*

PLAYING FAVORITES

CANDLE: *Cire Trudon's Abd El Kader. The soft minty scent both warms and freshens the room.*

COCKTAIL: *Apple Cider Mimosas.*

CHAMPAGNE: *Perrier-Jouët. I love it as much for the bottle as for the Champagne.*

FLOWER: *Peonies from my garden.*

FOOD: *Paella. As a bonus, it is a meal that can be cooked while chatting with friends and family.*

GUEST SOAP: *Diptyque softening hand wash. It has a delicate scent that is great for both men and women.*

HORS D'OEUVRE: *Radishes with salty butter and fleur de sel. If I am feeling really creative, I serve them in terra-cotta pots.*

LINENS: *Leontine and any collection of vintage French linens in sun-washed colors.*

WINE, RED: *The Prisoner. It is a blend that pleases a lot of palates.*

WINE, WHITE: *Sancerre Clos de Beaujeu is crisp and great for brunch or light dinners.*

WINE, ROSÉ: *Finca Wölffer rosé. I love summer nights at Wölffer Estate Vineyard in Sagaponack, New York.*

APPLE CIDER MIMOSAS

Serves 4

The mimosa is the archetypal weekend cocktail. This classic almost always features Champagne and orange juice. However, if you are looking to breathe new life into your Sunday morning standby, try it with apple cider—perfect for toasting the fall.

1 cup apple cider
1 dash bitters
1 bottle of cava, dry prosecco, or sparkling brut
4 apple slices

Fill four Champagne flutes one-quarter full with apple cider. Add 2 to 3 drops of bitters to each flute and top off with sparkling wine. Garnish each with a slice of apple.

Note: This drink pairs well with melon, brie, prosciutto, and criossants.

MOTHER'S DAY BRUNCH

Kimberly Schlegel Whitman

Brunch is a long-standing Southern tradition. It offers a moment to catch up, visit, and unwind. For lifestyle maven Kimberly Schlegel Whitman, Mother's Day weekend affords the perfect opportunity to indulge in such an occasion. It is an ideal time to spend a leisurely afternoon with her mother, sisters, and daughter. "Family means everything to me," Kimberly says with a smile. Her love of family is evidenced by the hundreds of photographs that greet all who enter her sprawling Dallas home. An iconic photo of friend Buzz Aldrin landing on the moon sent to commemorate the birth of her son includes a note that reads, "Welcome to this world."

Early summer in Texas sees plenty of pleasant weather, and today is no exception. For this festive affair, Kimberly creates an outdoor dining experience that is intimate, easy, and fun. The day before the brunch she set the table, arranged the flowers, and laid out all of the serving pieces. Deep yellow fretwork dinner napkins, terra-cotta pots brimming with flowers and ferns, and midcentury Ernestine Cannon butterfly and bamboo plates bring the white linen-covered table to life. "Organizing ahead of time helps you enjoy your guests," she offers.

She admits that gathering and arranging flowers is her favorite part of entertaining. "I find it so relaxing and therapeutic," she affirms. Even though Kimberly attended Catherine Muller's flower school in Paris and is well-versed in the intricacies of formal floral arranging, she is always experimenting. She is also known to change her mind on a whim. On the day of the brunch, she clips some daisies and tucks them into blue-and-white vases interspersed between the tiny terra-cotta pots. "I'm always looking for great containers for flowers. I love to hunt at auctions, flea markets, and estate sales," she says.

Her Mother's Day brunch is the perfect example of relaxed, high-low entertaining—an easy cheese board, assorted pastries served on fine, linen napkins, delicate green glasses filled with freshly squeezed orange juice, sparkling water, and copious amounts of crisp, cold Champagne make everyone happy. A simple-to-prepare breakfast casserole is the star of the show. "I love a great casserole. It pleases the palate of every generation at the table," Kimberly shares. "Not to mention that no one wants to slave over a hot stove in May." It's the perfect way to enjoy the day and be a guest at her own party, especially on Mother's Day.

MAKE IT EASY
CHEESE BOARD
BASICS

Kimberly's party go-to is a great cheese board. While there are no hard and fast rules when it comes to preparing a cheese board, these simple suggestions will help you prepare a spread that is sure to impress your guests.

SELECT: *Choose one cheese from each of the four cheese categories:*
Aged—cheddar, Gruyère, or Gouda
Blue—Maytag or Stilton
Hard—Manchego or Parmigiano-Reggiano
Soft—Brie or Camembert

Allow 4 to 6 ounces per person. Include a variety of cheese textures and flavors to keep the selection interesting and offer the widest appeal to different tastes.

ACCOMPANIMENTS: *Pair your cheese selections with an assortment of fresh fruits, dried fruits, nuts, and condiments. Select food that will complement the cheese. A few suggestions include olives, olive tapenade, balsamic vinegar, dried apricots, grapes, fig preserves, quince paste, chutney, chorizo, prosciutto, water biscuits, a crusty baguette, slices of artisanal rye bread, marcona almonds, and grainy mustard.*

PREPARE: *Cheese is more flavorful at room temperature. Remove the cheeses from the refrigerator one hour before serving. Slice some of each cheese to make it easier for your guests. Place the condiments and accompaniments in small serving dishes.*

ARRANGE: *Arrange your cheeses on a large platter, marble slab, or wooden board. Place a few of the accompaniments on the cheese board. Serve bread and crackers in a separate basket or bowl.*

CASSEROLE CONFIDENTIAL

Make certain that your dish is oven safe. If a dish or pan is not marked ovenproof, it may shatter at high temperatures. Note that decorative dishes may contain lead.

Spray casserole pans with a nonstick cooking spray for a fast and easy cleanup.

For most baking situations, the middle rack will cook and bake food more evenly. Do keep in mind that this rule applies only when you are baking on one rack at a time.

If you like a crisp top, do not cover your casserole. If you use aluminum foil to cover your casserole, place the shiny side down so that it retains heat rather than deflecting it.

BREAKFAST CASSEROLE

Serves 6 to 8

Looking for an easy and delicious recipe to add to your repertoire? Look no further than this savory casserole. This make-ahead dish is perfect for a holiday gathering, a birthday breakfast, or a simple, satisfying spread.

2 tablespoons extra-virgin olive oil
1 red bell pepper, diced
1 green bell pepper, diced
1 yellow bell pepper, diced
1 yellow onion, diced
2 cups fresh spinach, chopped
2 cups sourdough bread cubes
1 cup whole milk
½ cup heavy cream
6 large eggs
1 teaspoon ground cumin
1 teaspoon ground cayenne pepper
1 tablespoon hot sauce
Salt and freshly ground black pepper to taste
¼ cup fresh baby spinach leaves, for garnish
½ cup halved cherry tomatoes, for garnish

Preheat the oven to 350°F. Heat the oil in a medium skillet over medium-high heat. Add the peppers and onions. Sauté until the peppers are soft and the onions are translucent, about 5 minutes.

In a large bowl, mix the spinach with the bread. Spread the mixture evenly in the bottom of a 9 by 13-inch casserole dish.

In a large bowl, whisk the milk, heavy cream, eggs, cumin, cayenne, hot sauce, and salt and pepper. Stir in the sautéed peppers and onions. Pour the mixture over the spinach and bread layer. Bake in the preheated oven until set, about 30 minutes. Garnish with spinach leaves and cherry tomatoes.

BREAKFAST
IN THE GARDEN
Sarah Eilers

O n a cool spring day Sarah Eilers whips up a batch of hot biscuits and throws open her doors for a midmorning get-together. An intimate courtyard and blooming garden are the perfect setting for gathering a group of girlfriends. Assembling friends for breakfast proves a novel departure from the typical dinner party. "So often breakfast is overlooked as an opportunity to entertain," Sarah laments. "Some of my most memorable meals have occurred over breakfast."

Today, Houston's unseasonable weather is generously accommodating. Budding flowers, crisp scents, and joyful sounds create a perfect atmosphere. Bright green foxtail ferns, blooming oakleaf hydrangeas, and fragrant gardenias and camellias add an additional punch of color and fragrance.

For the interior designer and devoted gardener, the pleasure of entertaining starts with pondering the menu and considering foods that will fit the occasion and delight her guests. "Buttermilk biscuits are my favorite. Especially when they are doughy on the inside and crispy on the outside," she confesses. After tasting an assortment of sweet and savory biscuits from Ouisie's Table, the self-proclaimed bread enthusiast was inspired to find the perfect recipe for this party. "The secret is White Lily flour," she shares. Mimosas and a biscuit bar complete with all of the accompaniments—butter, jams, and jellies— greet her guests. Sliced Smithfield smoked ham, sausage gravy, fruit salad with mint and crème fraîche, quiche, yogurt, and muffins round out the mix.

An avid collector, Sarah has only to open the doors of her china cabinets, butler's pantry, and linen closet to set a stunning table. She often uses items from around the house and tucks poppies, tulips, and sunflowers into small blue vases, silver cups, and cachepots. Whether the table is set with treasured china, new linens, or a mix of antique objects, each meal is an opportunity to indulge her love of entertaining and design. "Setting the table for a party can be just as creative and personal as devising the menu," she says.

Under a large Chinese elm tree, two tables are set for twelve. Wispy, weeping branches shield guests from the bright morning sun. Custom tablecloths in shades of spring green and cobalt blue, fashioned from Brunschwig & Fils Zenobia fabric, lay the foundation for an artful tabletop. Bernardaud porcelain plates, adorned with blue cornflowers and laurel bands, marry with green Depression sherbet glasses, mouth-blown blue stemware, and mossy-green Leontine Linens.

No detail is overlooked. Stacks of books sit atop Chinese garden stools. Cashmere throws are folded at the foot of each chaise lounge, and a pashmina wrap is gently draped on the back of each chair should guests need an added layer of protection from the wind. By the time everyone arrives, Sarah is ready to relax with her friends.

SARAH'S SOUTHERN BISCUITS

Makes 8 biscuits

Southern biscuits are flaky, fluffy, buttery, and absolutely delicious. It is important that cold ingredients remain cold. When the biscuits hit a hot oven, you will get a quick rise with lots of layers. White Lily flour is a Southern favorite— the soft wheat is low in gluten and protein. King Arthur self-rising flour is a good option as well.

1 stick (8 tablespoons) cold unsalted butter, cubed, plus more for lightly coating the baking sheet
2 ¼ cups self-rising flour, preferably White Lily, plus extra for the work surface
1 ¼ cups cold buttermilk
2 tablespoons unsalted butter, melted

Preheat the oven to 450°F. Lightly butter a baking sheet or jelly-roll pan and set aside.

In a large bowl, cut the cold butter into the flour until the mixture resembles coarse crumbs. Make a well in the center of the mixture and pour in the buttermilk. Stir just until the dough comes together. The dough will be very sticky. Cover the bowl with plastic wrap and refrigerate for 10 minutes.

Turn the dough out onto a lightly floured work surface. Using floured hands, gently knead and fold the dough over on itself 5 or 6 times.

Pat or lightly roll the dough into a ¾-inch-thick rectangle. Cut the dough with a floured 2 ½-inch biscuit cutter. Place the cut biscuits on the lightly buttered baking sheet or jelly-roll pan. The biscuits should be touching.

Bake the biscuits until lightly browned, 13 to 15 minutes. Brush the tops with the melted butter. Serve right away.

BREAKFAST CHEAT SHEET

BEVERAGES: *orange juice, grapefruit juice, coffee, and tea*

BISCUITS: *homemade*

BUTTER: *organic, salted*

CANDLES: *Thymes*

CHINA: *Bernardaud Limoges (pattern: Barbeaux)*

FLOWERS: *sunflowers, white tulips, ranunculus, poppies, golden dewdrops*

GUEST SOAP: *Summer Hill by Crabtree & Evelyn*

JAMS: *homemade apricot and fig preserves*

LINENS: *Leontine Linens*

PROSECCO: *La Marca*

STEMWARE: *Artland Iris*

STERLING FLATWARE: *Antique Fiddle Thread by Frank Smith*

TABLECLOTHS: *Brunschwig & Fils*

TEA: *English breakfast*

BRIDGE AND BRUNCH
Grace Kaynor

Mention the game of bridge and most people envision their grandmothers playing cards in a living room that appears to have been decorated by June Cleaver. However, interior designer and bridge aficionado Grace Kaynor just might change your mind. An elegant game with many layers, bridge is filled with strategy and tactics—part math, part logic, and part reason. Bill Gates and Warren Buffett are both self-proclaimed enthusiasts. And despite its highbrow image, bridge was the perfect populist pastime during the war years. Not only is it both sociable and stimulating, but also the only expense involved is the purchase of a deck of cards.

The game offers a great excuse for Grace to bring like-minded friends together and host an intimate brunch. For the midday menu, she opts for recipes that are easy to prepare. Cheddar cheese biscuits, tarragon chicken salad sandwiches, a sweet and salty trail mix, and Lynchburg lemonade are all great standbys.

Grace's 1850s Greek Revival house in the New Orleans Garden District is her favorite place to hold a bridge get-together, and she is especially fond of entertaining in the charming solarium. Once a dowdy home office, the room was transformed by the designer, who cleverly lined its walls and ceiling in ornate pale blue latticework. A large window behind the sofa lets in rays of sunlight that are reflected in the mirrors behind the trellises. Glimpses of greenery from the courtyard and beyond are also returned in the reflection. Black and white cushion-cut ceramic tiles offer a modern and low-maintenance alternative to costly marble flooring.

Working with local craftsmen, Grace spent four years fastidiously restoring and preserving the historic 170-year-old mansion. Walls were removed, entryways were widened, and rooms were opened up and reconfigured to create grand spaces for both family affairs and entertaining. Towering thirteen-foot ceilings, elaborate moldings, and massive fireplace mantels were just a few of the elements that drew the hostess to the house.

Grace and noted architect Davis Jahncke, Jr. made use of all available space. Beneath the floating staircase, the pair fashioned a functioning butler's pantry. To shake things up, Grace opted for a whimsically patterned malachite wall covering. The exquisite saturated green is a playful background to crisp white linens, polished silver, porcelain trays, and platters—everything she needs for a bridge party and other occasions. "I set out to preserve a historic house, but in the end the house preserved me," smiles Grace.

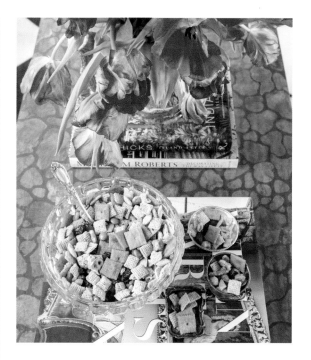

LYNCHBURG LEMONADE

Serves 1

Lynchburg lemonade is named for Lynchburg, Tennessee, home of the Jack Daniel's distillery. It is one of the most popular mixed drinks in the South and has many fans across the United States. Tart, cool, and refreshing, the cocktail is a great summertime pick-me-up. Grace makes her version with fresh ingredients.

1 ½ ounces (3 tablespoons) whiskey, preferably
   Jack Daniel's Old No. 7
½ ounce (1 tablespoon) triple sec
½ ounce (1 tablespoon) freshly squeezed
   lemon juice
3 ounces (¼ cup plus 2 tablespoons)
   fresh lemonade
1 lemon or orange wedge

Fill a highball glass with ice cubes. Pour the whiskey over the ice. Add the triple sec, lemon juice, and lemonade. Stir to combine, then garnish with the lemon or orange wedge.

GRACE'S PARTY MIX

Serves 4 to 6

Grace's modern-day version of the original 1950s Chex party mix is a sweet and salty combination of several of her favorite snacks.

2 cups Chex Mix traditional snack mix
2 cups Cheez-It hot and spicy snack crackers
2 cups Planters trail mix (nuts, seeds, and cranberries)
1 cup pretzel sticks
1 cup M&M's milk chocolate minis

Mix all the ingredients together in a large bowl. Store the mixture in an airtight container until ready to serve.

THE BUTLER'S PANTRY

Historically, a butler's pantry was a space dedicated to counting, polishing, and storing silver. Such spaces have experienced a resurgence in popularity in recent years. For parties, a butler's pantry can also be used as a self-serve bar. And bigger is not necessarily better. Grace's own home proves that a small, perfectly proportioned pantry can be both functional as well as visually exciting.

LOVELY
LUNCHES

A LIVELY LUNCH
AT THE RANCH
Lynn Wyatt

When Lynn Wyatt enters a room the atmosphere palpably shifts. Her serene presence, infectious laugh, and down-to-earth personality instantly put people at ease. For five decades the hostess has been a social icon and international philanthropist. She can effortlessly host a dazzling dinner for Plácido Domingo or mix a mean margarita with the greatest of ease. Much like her famed tequila cocktail, the hostess is unforgettable. It is no surprise that she has counted among her closest friends some of the world's greatest entertainers, novelists, artists, and cultural figures, including Andy Warhol, Elton John, Grace Kelly, Estée Lauder, and Sarah Ferguson, the Duchess of York.

Lynn loves to entertain at her family's South Texas ranch, Tasajillo, a name conceived by the former first lady of Texas, Nellie Connally. The 36,000-square-foot main house sits respectfully in the landscape. Surrounded by centuries-old mesquite trees, cacti, succulents, and palm trees, the house and region have a flavor of their own. Despite its size, the hacienda is cozy, comfortable, and well loved. A division of Wyatt Ranches, the property was acquired in the mid-1960s.

From the great room, a massive wall of glass and wooden doors with graceful archways leads to an inviting interior courtyard. Two long arcades flank the pool and run the length of the house. A vast covered porch with an outdoor bar offers a reprieve from the sun and functions as an alfresco living room. It is a relaxing place to gather, gossip, regroup, and have fun. It is also the perfect spot for appetizers. Homemade pico de gallo and guacamole stave off everyone's appetite.

Round equipale tables and barrel chairs are picture-perfect for the late lunch. Crafted from tanned pigskin and Mexican cedar strips, each piece of equipale furniture is made by hand. Colorful cushions add a touch of coziness to the rustic design and beckon guests to come dine. Staying true to the local cuisine, Lynn devises a menu that reflects the province and the culture.

Hundreds of metal lanterns, crafted with hand-blown glass, cradle small candles. Ruby ball cactuses, also known as red cap cactuses, add texture and color to the table. Uriarte Talavera Mexican pottery in shades of green and brown set against an ivory white background, harmonizes with mesquite grilled beef tenderloin and bundles of asparagus spears bound with bright carrot ribbons. "I love a pretty table," Lynn muses, "but it's the people that make the party. You can have perfect lighting, great music, fantastic food, you name it, but it's still all about the people."

Ronda

LYNN LOVES

CANDLES: *A. I. Root Company French vanilla*

CAVIAR: *beluga*

CHAMPAGNE: *Perrier-Jouët and Moët & Chandon Imperial Brut*

COOKBOOK: La Cocina Mexicana *by Marilyn Tausend*

CRYSTAL: *Baccarat*

DINNERWARE: *Uriarte Talavera pottery from Puebla, Mexico*

FLOWERS: *white orchids and yellow roses*

GUEST SOAP: *Gilchrist & Soames Reserve Collection*

PANTRY ESSENTIALS: *hearts of palm, sweet and spicy barbecue sauce, roasted pineapple and habanero sauce, homemade corn tortilla chips, and South Texas natural honey*

STATIONERY: *Crane & Co.*

TEA: *Vietnam imperial oolong*

TEQUILA: *Patrón and Don Julio 1942 Anejo*

WINE, RED: *Château La Tour du Pin Figeac*

WINE, WHITE: *Meursault Louis Jadot Côte d'Or, Lucien Albrecht, Viña Soledad Blanco*

LETI'S MARGARITA

Serves 1

The beginnings of this humble drink are a mystery. While several stories circulate, many believe Texas socialite Margaret (aka Margarita) Sames first mixed one up at a house party in Acapulco in 1948. Despite the ambiguity, the tequila, orange liqueur, and lime juice concoction is a staple at the Wyatt ranch.

Salt for rims, optional
1 ½ ounces (3 tablespoons) gold tequila
½ ounce (1 tablespoon) triple sec, preferably Cointreau
4 ounces (½ cup) Sweet-and-Sour Mix (recipe follows)
1 slice lime, for garnish
1 slice lemon, for garnish

If using salt, salt the rim of a chilled margarita glass.

Pour the tequila, triple sec, and mix into a cocktail shaker filled with ice cubes. Shake well. Strain the margarita into the prepared glass, with or without fresh ice. Garnish with both a lime and lemon slice.

SWEET-AND-SOUR MIX

Makes 8 cups

3 cups water
3 cups sugar
2 cups freshly squeezed lemon juice
2 cups freshly squeezed lime juice

Combine the water and sugar in a large saucepan. Stir over medium heat until the sugar dissolves. Bring to a boil and remove from the heat.

Allow the syrup to cool. Then mix the syrup, lemon juice, and lime juice in a pitcher. Cover with plastic wrap and refrigerate until the mixture is cold.

Note: The Sweet-and-Sour Mix can be made one week in advance. Cover with plastic wrap and keep chilled.

LUPITA'S PICO DE GALLO

Makes 3 cups

Pico de gallo, also referred to as salsa fresca, is a fresh, uncooked mixture of chopped tomatoes, onions, cilantro, chilies, lime juice, and salt that is chunky by nature. Like guacamole, pico de gallo should be served with plenty of tortilla chips.

1 ½ pounds plum tomatoes, chopped
1 medium white onion, diced
½ cup finely chopped cilantro
1 jalapeño pepper, finely diced (remove seeds and membranes for a milder salsa)
Freshly squeezed juice of 1 lime
Salt to taste

Add the tomatoes, onion, cilantro, diced pepper, and lime juice to a medium bowl. Season with salt. Set the salsa aside for 30 minutes. After 30 minutes, stir the salsa to distribute the juices. Taste and adjust with more salt if needed. Serve with tortilla chips.

Note: Pico de gallo can be stored for up to two days in an airtight container in the refrigerator.

GUACAMOLE

Makes 3 ½ cups

Avocados, sea salt, lime juice, and cilantro make the perfect guacamole. This astounding avocado dip was first developed by the Aztecs in what is now Mexico. A favorite of modern Mexican cuisine, this green goddess is now an integral part of American gastronomy and Lynn's entertaining repertoire. Serve with plenty of tortilla chips for dipping.

4 large ripe avocados
1 teaspoon sea salt
2 tablespoons freshly squeezed lime juice
¼ cup cilantro leaves, finely chopped
¼ teaspoon freshly ground black pepper

Cut the avocados in half and remove the pits. Spoon the flesh of the avocados into a mixing bowl.

Roughly mash the avocados with a fork. Do not over mash. The guacamole should be a bit chunky.

Stir in the salt, lime juice, cilantro, and pepper. Serve immediately, as guacamole turns brown if it sits for too long.

A NEW ORLEANS-INSPIRED FEAST

Katie Scott

For the Scott household, every occasion presents an opportunity to weave together an enjoyable cast of characters. Grandparents, children, neighbors, nieces, nephews, and friends—all are welcome. For New Orleans native and designer Katie Scott, family, fun, and food rule the day. Both Katie and her husband, Stanton, were born and raised in Louisiana. Cooking is in their DNA. Katie's mother was hired by Emeril Lagasse to cater his engagement party. "Growing up, our house —especially the kitchen—was like Grand Central Station with a revolving door. It never fazed my mom; it only fed her soul." Likewise, food and family feed and inspire Katie.

On a lazy Sunday afternoon the Scotts' Houston home is the nexus for a Crescent City–inspired lunch and bloody mary bar. In New Orleans the laissez-faire approach to life is de rigueur. However, weekend meals and bloody marys are taken seriously. "We pride ourselves on concocting astounding bloodies."

Her vibrant and colorful dwelling has as much personality as her party and guest list. Eclectic art, humorous photography, unique ceramics, interesting antiques, eye-popping serving pieces, and children populate the space. Everything is stylish, yet family-friendly. An eclectic mix of traditional pieces and unexpected bursts of color keep the aesthetic grounded, sophisticated, and casual. The bright and elegantly appointed kitchen and dining room are the hub and heart of the home. The sweeping space spills onto a large sunroom with a forty-foot wall of windows looking out to a courtyard.

Katie's chic black-and-white dining room and large kitchen island offer the perfect spots for an expansive spread. The buffet, featuring French-inspired Creole cooking, seems endless with stuffed artichokes, jumbo lump crabmeat, shrimp cocktail, Belgian endive with blue cheese, toasted walnuts, spiced pecans, aged cheeses, honeycombs, figs, toast points, French bread, and chocolate.

In the living room, an antique commode doubles as the bloody mary bar, while a bevy of age-appropriate beverages chill in large ice buckets. Bottles of Ramune Japanese soda, in a variety of unusual flavors, including wasabi and bubble gum, provide both refreshment and entertainment. Glass bottles, cleverly sealed with marble stoppers, delight younger guests.

Even the tiniest visitors are treated to Katie's style and hospitality. Today, the open-air space is reserved strictly for kids to play and dine alfresco. Bright neon Alexandra von Furstenberg acrylic napkin rings and beveled-edge placemats charge the space and electrify the outdoor dining table.

Katie is so lighthearted one might mistake her for a guest. Though relaxed, she quietly supervises everything, making certain that her guests are happy and comfortable. "Just like my mom, I love to spoil my family and friends."

THE BLOODY MARY BAR

A bloody mary bar is a great idea for a large weekend gathering. Whether your guests favor a tall tangy version of this beverage or an extra hot shot, they will enjoy mixing up their own drink. Best yet, it frees up the hosts from bar duty.

MIX: *We use Debutante Farmer bloody mary mix. It is seasoned to perfection. Be sure to offer several brands of vodka.*

SEASON: *Tabasco and Worcestershire sauces are classic partners. A few others to include: celery salt, garlic salt, caraway seeds, black pepper, smoked paprika, or horseradish.*

GARNISH: *Don't forget the garnishes. While celery is the go-to garnish, I also love to offer pickled green beans, pickled okra, crispy bacon, cherry tomatoes, blue cheese–stuffed olives, and lemon wedges.*

CHILL: *Freeze some of the bloody mary mix in ice cube trays. It will chill your drink without watering it down.*

BLOODY MARY

Serves 1

While the exact origins of the bloody mary is murky, cocktail historians generally agree that a bartender by the name of Fernand "Pete" Petiot, concocted a basic version in the early 1920s while employed at Harry's New York Bar in Paris. After Prohibition, Pete brought the drink to the King Cole Bar at the St. Regis Hotel in Manhattan. While at the St. Regis, he dressed up the tomato-juice creation with horseradish, Tabasco, lemon juice, and celery salt—the drink we know today.

2 ounces (¼ cup) vodka
8 ounces (1 cup) bloody mary mix,
   preferably Debutante Farmer
1 teaspoon Worcestershire sauce
2 or 3 dashes hot pepper sauce, such as Tabasco
1 pinch salt
1 pinch freshly ground black pepper
1 teaspoon freshly squeezed lemon juice
½ cup ice cubes
1 stalk celery
1 lemon wedge

In a highball glass, stir together the vodka, bloody mary mix, Worcestershire sauce, hot sauce, salt, and pepper. Add lemon juice and mix well. Fill the glass with ice. Garnish with a celery stalk and a lemon wedge, and serve.

A Scandinavian smorgasbord is a thing of beauty. A long table laden with smoked meats, gravlax, cheeses, pâtés, and bread epitomizes Nordic cuisine. Simply defined, it is an extensive array of hors d'oeuvres, salads, cheeses, fish, fruits, and sweets. Nevertheless, Cris Briger makes simple look endlessly extraordinary.

In the Briger home in Washington, D.C., life is celebrated at the table and Cris is forever prepared. Bottles of Champagne are always chilled, and ready-to-bake gougères, from Formaggio Kitchen in Boston, inhabit the freezer. The light, savory pastry bites, made with imported Comté cheese, are a family favorite. Once they are in the oven, they billow into flaky shells with soft and savory centers. "A gougère is the perfect complement to a glass of Veuve Clicquot," Cris surmises.

The art of living well, married with a dose of practicality, imbues Cris's entertaining philosophy. "I buy in bulk, and if I have eggs and butter I can make a meal for friends in a pinch. Omelets, egg salad, deviled eggs, scrambled eggs. It's endless," says the designer and antiques dealer, whose favorite app is Instacart.

Her wit and approach to life also apply to her design aesthetic. Antique dining chairs covered in varying shades of pale blue fabric stand out against creamy white walls. A pair of early Baguès sconces takes the place of a traditional chandelier. A polychrome carved Turk, bearing a single candle, and unornamented Christmas trees provide an ethereal feel.

For this December luncheon every surface is given full attention, including the floors. Following an ancient custom, bay laurel leaves are scattered over the ground to symbolize the beauty of the season. Tradition also dictates writing holiday wishes on the dried leaves before they are crushed in the hope that those desires will be fulfilled. However, Cris uses the leaves in their natural state to provide an added layer of magic and a beautiful smell. "It's just a pleasure for all the senses. Unexpected things make your guests feel as though you have thought of everything solely for their enjoyment," she smiles. "But do be careful. The leaves can be slippery."

Offering a large plate to each guest, she instructs everyone to help themselves to the assortment on the serving platters. Flickering votives and starched snow-white linens welcome friends to the table. The inviting setting offers a reprieve from the seasonal hustle and bustle, while encouraging relaxation and conversation. Never a hostess to dictate conversation or the flow of the table, Cris's legendary gatherings can last for hours, often inspiring a game of charades.

No Briger get-together is complete without rich chocolate crème marquise. Cris prefers Alice B. Toklas's version. "Florence Van der Kemp, wife of Gerald Van der Kemp, once the curator of Versailles, said to always end a dinner party with something chocolate. After all, that's why it's called a dinner party. It is a rule that I have always followed."

PATTERN PLAY

Cofounder of Get the Gusto in West Palm Beach, Florida, Cris is a master at mixing patterns, art, antiques, dishes, and linens. Whether it is interiors or tabletops, her suggestions make mixing fun.

MIX: *Combine large patterns with smaller prints in complementary colors. This gives a cohesive look and pulls everything together. Consider eggplants in a garden—shades of dark purple and earthy greens are a perfect marriage. Choose a larger scale for the walls and find complementary small patterns and colors to disperse throughout the room.*

GO BIG: *Use one pattern on the walls, draperies, and upholstered furniture. It makes a daring statement in any space, especially small areas like entryways, powder rooms, and hallways.*

SELECT: *Pick one color palette that you love and let it be your guide; the rest will follow. Don't be afraid. Most important, have fun with checks, stripes, and paisley. The possibilities are endless. My favorite fabric houses include Raoul Textiles, Cowtan & Tout, Manuel Canovas, Colefax and Fowler, Hines & Company, Jasper Fabrics, Ronda Carman Fine Fabrics, and Les Indiennes.*

CHOCOLATE CRÈME MARQUISE

Serves 6

Dark chocolate is king among chocolate-lovers. This decadent, melt-in-your-mouth showstopper, adapted from Alice B. Toklas's recipe, requires only chocolate, butter, and eggs and doesn't need baking, making it easy to prepare for a dinner party. A top-quality chocolate is key.

6 ounces 70 percent dark or semisweet chocolate, roughly chopped
1 stick (8 tablespoons) unsalted butter, cut into pieces
6 large eggs, separated

Place the chocolate in a heatproof bowl. Suspend the bowl over a low, simmering pot of water. Do not allow the base of the bowl to touch the water. Stir the chocolate until it softens and is almost completely melted.

Add the butter one piece at a time. Stir between each addition until melted.

Add the egg yolks one at a time. Continually stir in the same direction. Once the yolks are incorporated, remove the bowl from the heat.

Beat the egg whites in a clean bowl until stiff peaks form. Fold the egg whites into the chocolate mixture. Divide the chocolate mixture among 6 individual chocolate pots, or pour into a terrine mold. Cover the mold or chocolate pots with plastic wrap and refrigerate at least 12 hours before serving.

AN ALL-AMERICAN AFFAIR
Ware Porter

There is a down-home lavishness about Ware Porter. Interior decorator, shop owner, host, cook, and flower designer—this bon vivant can do it all. The discerning Southerner is a man of many talents. An Alabama native, he now calls New Orleans home. The gracious and gregarious host credits his mother for many of his attributes. "Growing up, our home always had an open-door policy. There was always more than enough room for everyone at the table. Roaring fires, cocktails, good food, and lots of people were the norm," Ware fondly recalls.

Like his mom, Ware is an affable individual, a trait that quickly ingratiates him with new neighbors and friends alike. To christen the Garden District Creole camelback Ware shares with his partner, Jordi Land, they opened their abode for a late-afternoon affair. The term "camelback" refers to the second floor at the rear of the structure. The twelve-foot-wide rectangular residence is also a "shotgun" house, so named because the rooms are arranged one behind the other so that a shot fired through the front door would exit out the rear door without touching a wall.

Shortly after moving in, Ware transformed the front room into a dining-room-cum-library. The laid-back, stylish space is grounded in classical proportions and whimsical sensibilities. Chartreuse bookcases flank one of two fireplaces, while a circular table takes center stage. It is draped with Quadrille Bali Hai fabric, whose color perfectly complements the blue interior of the shelves.

A mixture of patterns adds texture, depth, and interest to the place settings. Garden roses, embellished rattan chargers, and Mottahedeh Tobacco Leaf china marry with lots of silver. Ware's father started giving him silver when he was still in high school, and he has been collecting ever since. "I especially adore my Verdura silver shells. They are migratory objects you will find on my coffee table or my dining table. They are so naturally beautiful. Silver is a part of my Southern roots."

On this occasion, the host opts to adapt the celebrated meatloaf that was a signature of American fashion designer Bill Blass. Blass was known to serve it for dinner in his bucolic 1770 Connecticut house, originally built as a tavern. Often Ware and Jordi present the cherished dish family-style alongside carrots, mashed potatoes, gravy, and lots of Champagne. "Food always tastes better served with endless Champagne," Ware smiles.

COLLECTING SILVER

GETTING STARTED: *Before you start collecting, you need to understand the different types of silver. First, solid silver is too soft for regular use, so most of what you will find on the market is either sterling silver or silver-plated.*

Sterling silver consists of 92.5 percent solid silver and 7.5 percent other metals. It is most durable and will last for centuries if cared for properly. Almost all nineteenth- and twentieth-century sterling silver pieces bear clear marks of the word "sterling" or the number 925.

A thin layer of silver covers a base metal for silver-plated items. The most commonly used metal base is nickel. These items are marked with the words "silver-plate" or "electroplate," or, in some cases, the initials "EPNS" for electro-plated nickel silver.

A piece that is not marked with the word "sterling" or the number 925 is unlikely to be sterling silver. Pieces of American silver dating to the period after 1860 generally bear the "sterling" mark. Before 1860, makers usually marked their work with their names or initials. Such early American silver is rare.

HALLMARKS: *To identify your silver piece, start by finding the mark. Makers' marks, or hallmarks, are the tiny stamped initials found on the undersides or backsides of most silver pieces. If you cannot read a mark clearly, dip a cotton swab in a gentle silver polish and brush it over the mark. This will remove surface tarnish, allowing the mark to be read more easily. A great source for silver identification is the* Online Encyclopedia of Silver Marks, Hallmarks, & Makers' Marks: *www.925-1000.com.*

KEEP IT CLEAN: *Cleaning silver is easy. Always use a good polish, such as Goddard's silver polish foam or Hagerty silver-smiths' polish. When silver is not on display, it is best to store it in an airtight environment. This will also help to prevent dents and scratches. Washing by hand is recommended.*

BILL BLASS'S MEATLOAF

Serves 4 to 6

Ware adapted his bacon-topped meatloaf recipe, an American classic, from a recipe attributed to another American classic—renowned clothing designer Bill Blass. Known for dressing First Lady Nancy Reagan and other members of society, Blass reportedly loved simple fare and home-cooked meals. He was so closely associated with his meatloaf that his 2002 *New York Times* obituary made mention of it: "A man of robust but simple tastes who would go out of his way for a hamburger, Mr. Blass would serve guests his own meatloaf recipe, followed perhaps by lemon meringue pie. He always maintained, only partly in jest, 'My claim to immortality will be my meatloaf.'"

Vegetable oil for greasing the pan
3 tablespoons unsalted butter
½ cup chopped celery
1 yellow onion, chopped
2 pounds lean ground beef
½ pound ground veal
½ pound ground pork
¼ cup chopped flat-leaf parsley
⅓ cup sour cream
½ cup soft breadcrumbs
¼ teaspoon dried thyme
¼ teaspoon dried marjoram
¼ teaspoon dried oregano
Kosher salt and freshly ground black pepper
   to taste
1 large egg
1 tablespoon Worcestershire sauce
½ cup chili sauce, preferably Heinz
2 tablespoons spicy brown mustard
4 slices bacon

Preheat the oven to 350°F. Lightly grease an 8 by 4-inch loaf pan and set aside.

Place the butter in a heavy skillet and melt over medium heat. Add the celery and onion and sauté until soft. Transfer to a large mixing bowl and allow to cool.

When the mixture has cooled, add the meats, parsley, sour cream, breadcrumbs, thyme, marjoram, oregano, salt, and pepper to the bowl. In a separate small bowl, whisk the egg with the Worcestershire sauce and add to the meat mixture. Using a wooden spoon or your hands, combine the mixture and mold into a loaf.

Place the loaf in the prepared pan. Mix the chili sauce with the mustard and spread on top of the loaf. Top with bacon slices, arranged lengthwise. Bake in the preheated oven until meatloaf is firm and nicely browned and the bacon is crisp, about 1 hour. Allow to cool in the pan for 5 minutes, then unmold, slice, and serve.

LUNCH ON LONG ISLAND
Tricia Foley

Designer, habitual hostess, and lifestyle doyenne Tricia Foley is a master of effortlessness. On a sunny Sunday afternoon, light floods her Long Island home. Inside, the interiors are composed of varying shades of white and pops of color from nature—a signature style that she also applies to entertaining. As she steps onto her deck, white birds glided across the marsh on their way to Great South Bay.

After living in a circa 1845 home, and another built in 1820, Tricia was ready for a change. While visiting friends, she stumbled upon a twenty-five-year-old dilapidated two-story structure designed by local architect David Hatcher, best known for his modernist residences in the Pines neighborhood on Fire Island. Tricia took the plunge and brought the house back to life. Her home, nestled in the hamlet of Brookhaven amid a serene landscape, perfectly mirrors the tranquil interiors.

While Tricia awaits the arrival of her guests, she pours herself a glass of crisp, aromatic Sancerre and prepares lunch at her large kitchen counter. She then selects china, glasses, napkins, and pottery from her considerable collection of tabletop pieces. The former president of Wedgwood USA, she has been collecting china, silver, and linens since her high school days. "I have a serious tableware addiction," she laughs.

She carefully selects each object to create a special look that is perfect for the occasion. Rough, natural canvas covers a long table on the deck overlooking the water. Hefty white clamshells, votive candles, white glassware, and white vases accent the surface. "I love this look," Tricia confides. "It is natural, simple, and a bit quirky."

Her food is always seasonal and adaptable. A vegetarian, the hostess prefers pastas and salads for simple suppers. In the summer she is a fan of lemons, lemon juice, lemon zest, pine nuts, herbs, ravioli, and fresh vegetables from the local farmstand. A favorite standby is a plentiful antipasto platter. Tricia fills an oversized white tray with olives, provolone, prosciutto, fresh mozzarella, breadsticks, roasted peppers, and artichokes. She then places the dish in the kitchen with several varieties of wine so that guests can help themselves.

Though she possesses great cooking prowess, she does not make everything from scratch. "I am much more interested in setting the table and enjoying my company. I have no problem buying some of the food," she confesses. Her advice is to make a few things and purchase the rest. Lists are another secret weapon. For Tricia, making lists is a ritual. "I can't live without my lists. I always put them in my calendar so that I have a plan. A set plan makes entertaining a pleasure, not a chore."

And though the white space might make visitors think twice before accepting a glass of wine, Tricia is relaxed in her surroundings. Her laid-back, unflappable nature is contagious, instantly putting everyone at ease. There is no need to worry. "I bleach my slipcovers once a year," she smiles. Even laundry is a welcome ritual.

PLAYING FAVORITES

CANDLE: *Christian Tortu Forêt*

CHAMPAGNE: *Veuve Clicquot*

COCKTAIL: *Cinzano Bianco with San Pellegrino*

FLOWERS: *white peonies, white quince, and apple branches*

FOOD: *lemon pasta*

GUEST SOAP: *Penhaligon's Blenheim*

HORS D'OEUVRE: *Ottolenghi biscuits and white pistachios*

LINENS: *Society Limonta*

RED WINE: *Montepulciano*

ROSÉ: *Château Montaud*

WHITE WINE: *Maison Louis Latour Ardèche Chardonnay*

TRICIA ON WHITE

THE APPEAL: *White offers a serene background in which to live your life. A white palette also enables you to work with a multitude of styles and periods. Most often I employ pops of color from nature.*

GETTING WHITE RIGHT: *Using a single shade of white creates a dull, flat look. A room looks richer and has more depth when you use varying shades. Try semi-gloss paint for shine on trim and doors for more interest, dimension, and depth.*

KEEPING IT CLEAN: *Natural linens and canvas slipcovers are invaluable. You can simply throw them in the washing machine—a little bleach works wonders.*

SIMPLE CUCUMBER SOUP

Serves 4 as a first course or 2 as a main course

Chilled cucumber soup is an easy instant meal. It is one of the great rewards of summer. You could serve this soup with nothing more than some toasted pita and a salad. Its pale color looks as refreshing as it tastes. Top this with lump crabmeat, or keep it vegetarian. It is simple and tasty.

1 cucumber, seeded, peeled, and chopped
1 cup plain yogurt
1 cup low-fat sour cream
3 cloves garlic, chopped
Salt and freshly ground white pepper to taste
Leaves of 1 sprig fresh mint
Leaves of 2 sprigs fresh dill

In the bowl of a blender or a food processor fitted with the metal blade, combine the cucumber, yogurt, sour cream, garlic, salt, and pepper. Blend until smooth and adjust seasoning as needed.

Distribute the soup among small bowls and garnish with the herb leaves. The soup can be refrigerated for up to 2 days.

SUMMER HARVEST SALAD

Serves 4

You cannot let summer pass by without making this beautiful salad. It only calls for seven simple ingredients. Tomatoes and peaches are rock stars of the season and they take center stage here. The two combine perfectly with tender fresh mint, lemon, and olive oil. The result is a salad bursting with freshness.

15 small heirloom cherry tomatoes, halved
3 ripe peaches, pitted, peeled, and cut into 1-inch dice
Leaves of 2 to 3 tiny sprigs mint
Freshly squeezed juice of 1 lemon
2 tablespoons extra-virgin olive oil
Sea salt to taste
Freshly ground black pepper to taste

In a large bowl, gently mix the tomatoes and peaches. Add the mint leaves and lemon juice. Drizzle with the olive oil and toss gently.

Season to taste with salt and pepper. Serve immediately.

A BOUNTIFUL
BARN LUNCH
Amy Beth Cupp

Only Amy Beth Cupp could envision a 250-year-old dairy barn, which was later a machine repair shop, as a warm and welcoming abode. The artist, trained chef, and interior design consultant not only restored the longstanding structure, she and her husband, Scott, also acquired the adjacent inn in Warren, Connecticut.

The picturesque barn boasts exposed rough-hewn timbers and soaring twenty-nine-foot ceilings. To bring everything down to a human level, Amy devised an oversized island as the focal point, grounding the massive great room and dividing the kitchen from the open living and dining space. For the Parsons-trained floral designer, it provides the perfect place to indulge her love of flower arranging. During the holidays two full-sized Christmas trees take up residency on the colossal countertop. Once the balsam beauties come down, huge arrangements and vast blooming branches rotate throughout the seasons.

As friends arrive for a festive fall gathering, everyone congregates by the great room fireplace and in the kitchen. Black hutches that flank the island conceal dishes, stemware, serving plates, bowls, and silver. With the exception of the French Sully 2200 Lacanche range (a show-stopping masterpiece), everything is hidden from view. Two dishwashers, recycling bins, a coffee system, and a built-in refrigerator are fully integrated into the cabinets. "If the kitchen looks messy in an open plan, the entire house feels messy," Amy sighs. "Not to mention, what you see when you eat either enhances or impairs the experience."

A dreamy dining table awaits everyone's arrival. Buttery yellow Sferra linen napkins couple with orange Mottahedeh china and dark, natural-colored Perin-Mowen beeswax candles. It is the perfect palette for a rich mulligatawny soup composed of carrots, garbanzo beans, a Granny Smith apple, and chicken stock.

Amy's love of entertaining is evident to all who enter her home. From planning the menu and shopping for the food to styling the table and the flowers, she exquisitely executes her vision for the autumn gathering. Abundant food, delicious desserts, and interesting drinks are all hallmarks of this skilled hostess. Whether it is pumpkin bread dotted with chocolate chips or a brandy Alexander, served with a chocolate cookie straw, each is a delectable punctuation mark. "Nothing makes me happier than a candlelit dining table, well-fed friends, happy bellies, and being surrounded by my guests while carrying on and laughing."

MUSINGS ON
AGED OBJECTS

For Amy, well-loved items are far more desirable than those that are brand-new. She uses linen napkins at every meal, as she feels they are much nicer than bleached or dyed paper ones and also more eco-friendly. She advises, "Hang-dry linen napkins. That way they don't need to be pressed, as long as you are okay with a more relaxed vibe at the dinner table."

Amy professes that life is too short not to use the good china. She wholeheartedly believes that it enhances one's visual experience. Her mother-in-law once rolled her eyes when Amy served sandwiches on her wedding china—Rosenthal Versace Primavera. She said in her Knoxville drawl, "Amy serves saaaandwiches off the Verrrsaccce!"

We have all been told to skip the dishwasher if plates have a rim of gold, as heat can potentially remove metal details. It is a tip Amy chooses to ignore. "I don't sweat the idea that the gold might wear off. By the time it starts to fade, you will have gotten hundreds of uses out of your china. I would not give up using it only twice a year for all the gold rims in the world," she says.

Layer in pieces from different eras. Amy notes that she is particularly drawn to vintage objects that are difficult to place in history. They are the perfect bridge between rustic, modern, traditional, and today.

MULLIGATAWNY SOUP

Serves 6

If your only exposure to East Indian mulligatawny soup is a brief mention on an episode of Seinfeld, you are in for a delightful indulgence. Recipes vary greatly, and there is no definitive original version, but early references to it in English date as far back as 1784. Mulligatawny always tastes better the day after it is made, perfect for entertaining. Before guests arrive, reheat in a pot on the stovetop over medium-low heat.

1 tablespoon vegetable oil
½ tablespoon butter
1 cup roughly chopped carrot
½ cup diced onion
1 cup finely chopped celery
1 clove garlic, minced
¾ cup diced red bell pepper
½ turnip, peeled and chopped
1 Granny Smith apple, peeled, cored, and chopped
1 teaspoon curry powder
¼ teaspoon ground coriander
¼ teaspoon ground cloves
¼ teaspoon ground ginger
1 teaspoon salt
Freshly ground black pepper to taste

6 cups chicken stock
2 cups cooked chicken, shredded
One 29-ounce can garbanzo beans, drained and rinsed
¼ cup flaked unsweetened coconut

In a large soup pot, warm the vegetable oil and butter together over medium heat. Add the carrot and sauté for 2 minutes. Add the remaining vegetables and the apple. Sauté until tender, about 10 minutes.

Add the curry powder, coriander, cloves, ginger, salt, and pepper. Stir long enough to ensure that the spices have evenly coated the apple and the vegetables. Add 4 cups of the stock and bring to a boil. Then add the chicken.

In a food processor fitted with the metal blade, puree the garbanzo beans and the remaining 2 cups stock until smooth. Pour the puree into the soup and mix well. The garbanzo beans will slightly thicken the soup. Reduce the heat to a simmer and cook, uncovered, until the flavors have blended, about 8 to 10 minutes.

To serve, ladle hot soup into cups or bowls and garnish each with a few shavings of the coconut.

CHOCOLATE CHIP PUMPKIN BREAD

Makes 3 loaves

On Amy's twenty-fifth birthday, her mother presented her with a binder that contained handwritten tried-and-true recipes, including this pumpkin bread. The original called for walnuts, but Amy swapped them for chocolate chips. It is a family favorite.

1 cup vegetable oil, plus more for greasing the pans
3 cups sugar
4 large eggs, beaten
One 29-ounce can pumpkin puree
3 ½ cups all-purpose flour
1 teaspoon baking powder
2 teaspoons baking soda
2 teaspoons salt
½ teaspoon ground cloves
1 teaspoon ground cinnamon
1 teaspoon nutmeg
1 teaspoon allspice
⅔ cup water
One 12-ounce package Nestlé Toll House semisweet
   chocolate chips

Preheat the oven to 350°F. Grease three 8 by 4-inch loaf pans and set aside.

In a large bowl, combine 1 cup vegetable oil, the sugar, and eggs. Stir in the pumpkin puree.

In a separate large bowl, whisk together the flour, baking powder, baking soda, salt, and spices.

Combine the dry flour mixture with the wet pumpkin batter. Stir the dry ingredients into the pumpkin mixture just until blended. Add the water and continue stirring until everything is incorporated. Fold in the chocolate chips.

Divide the batter evenly among the prepared pans. Bake until a toothpick inserted in the center comes out clean, 60 to 65 minutes. Cool the breads in the pans on wire cooling racks for 10 minutes before removing the breads from the pans. Let rest on the racks right side up to cool completely.

GARDEN PARTIES

Sleeping dogs, fresh flowers, vine-covered walls, weathered terra-cotta pots, teak tables, blue-and-white pillows, scalloped umbrellas, and rattan baskets are all reminders of summer. These items also perfectly describe the alluring garden of Mac Hoak and Fred Perkins. Their charming home, lush lawn, and bucolic lifestyle are every bit as enviable as their iconic emporium, Mecox Gardens.

For Mac and Fred, one of the great pleasures of summer is a casual outdoor gathering with friends. After a long week of work and travel, they usually opt for simple suppers and quiet surroundings on the weekend. Unpretentious and stress-free fare makes it easy for the hosts and their guests to relax. "When it comes to summertime get-togethers, we tend to gravitate toward salads," Fred notes. "Everyone needs a few no-fail cold salad recipes and a great deli for takeout," Mac adds.

French doors, just off the kitchen of the main house, open onto an outdoor dining and living area, expanding the entertaining space. A sprawling yard separates their 1931 French-manor-style home from a shingled guesthouse. The two love to open the windows when they entertain. They also keep entrances unlocked, or at least ajar, so that when company arrives they can let themselves in and feel instantly at home.

For this summery menu Mac and Fred skip the main course and opt for a variety of salads, slices of crusty baguettes, rosé, lots of water, and an assortment of cookies from a local bakery. Herbs—basil, rosemary, and thyme—adorn the table, offering guests additional salad seasonings. Planter boxes filled with ice keep the salads cold and the late day heat at bay.

In keeping with the Mecox ethos, the table setting takes its lead from the surroundings and its inspiration from nature. Vignettes of potted succulents, garden ornaments, hurricane lamps, and large palm fronds take center stage. The menu celebrates seasonal offerings—chives, baby lettuce, carrots, corn, cucumbers, tomatoes, and fresh berries. For buffets, Mac and Fred adhere to the one plate and one fork philosophy. "We don't want to make it unduly hard for guests," Mac laughs. "There's just no need to juggle multiple bowls, plates, and flatware," Fred affirms.

CREATING A SALAD BUFFET

Choose recipes that you can make ahead and serve cold. Purchase both deli and bagged salads to make it easy, and rely on store-bought toppings to add additional flavor to the salad.

TOPPING IDEAS:
*Cured meats
Dried fruit, such as apricots, dried cranberries, raisins
Edamame
Fresh fruit, such as blueberries, chopped apples, grapes, pears, raspberries, strawberries
Nuts and seeds, such as pepitas, sesame, sunflower
Olives
Parmigiano Reggiano cheese
Pickled pepperoncini peppers
Sundried tomatoes
Whole grains, such as barley, couscous, farro, quinoa*

SALAD SUGGESTIONS:
*Green beans and new potatoes
Grilled chicken with blueberries
Grilled steak drizzled with balsamic vinegar
Heirloom tomatoes with pasta
Kale, quinoa, and feta cheese
Pasta with pesto and artichoke hearts
Peas and pasta
Roasted potatoes
Tarragon chicken with lemon*

SIMPLE VINAIGRETTE

Makes about 1 cup

1 small shallot, minced
1 small clove garlic, minced
2 teaspoons grainy or Dijon mustard
3 tablespoons white wine vinegar
1 tablespoon freshly squeezed lemon juice
1 tablespoon water
¾ cup extra-virgin olive oil
Kosher salt and freshly ground black pepper to taste

Combine the shallot, garlic, mustard, vinegar, lemon juice, and water in a large bowl and whisk to combine. Whisking continuously, slowly drizzle in the olive oil.

Season with salt and pepper. The vinaigrette will keep in the refrigerator for up to 2 weeks.

menu

~~~ salad
~~~ with apples
~~~ and oranges

~~~che

~~~ cake
and assorted tarts

A FRENCH-INSPIRED LUNCHEON

Suzanne Kasler

The ritual of dining is important to the French. Whether a meal is a simple lunch or a formal affair, equal attention is given to the food and presentation. Renowned interior designer Suzanne Kasler holds the same standards. It is her firm belief that designing a beautiful home and meal to share with family and friends makes for a fulfilling life. Likewise, few other pleasures rival enjoying meals together in such a setting.

Nearly every aspect of Suzanne's entertaining style is informed by her time spent in Paris. Her Regency-style Atlanta abode—wholly befitting any occasion—is a testament to her French-inspired taste. A large foyer spills onto a light-filled dining room, while glass and iron windows open to a covered porch and a garden beyond. The outdoor space is an idyllic location for an early autumn luncheon.

On a warm, breezy afternoon, whimsy and beauty abound. The palest of pink French rosés chill in an oversized sterling bowl. Koelreuteria branches rustle in the wind. Delicate wicker trays bursting with raspberries greet smiling guests. Miniature Louis Vuitton trunks, collected during Suzanne's travels, erupt with Pink Mondial and Quicksand roses. "In the early 1900s Louis Vuitton designed the Malle Fleurs trunk. They would fill the trunks with flowers and present them as gifts to their most important customers," she shares.

A long, wooden trestle table, nestled between rows of blooming Peegee hydrangea trees, sets the stage for the leisurely lunch. A grouping of vintage wrought-iron armchairs found in Avignon, France, offers an additional spot for guests to gather, relax, and catch up. When imagining her courtyard and gardens, Suzanne referenced the tailored gardens she fell in love with while living abroad. Creating beautiful spaces for guests to enjoy took top priority. "I believe your house absorbs positive energy from entertaining friends and family," she asserts.

This luncheon is proof positive that an elegant event need not be difficult. When a hectic work schedule proved challenging, the hostess reached out to Café Lapin, a local neighborhood bistro, to assist with the occasion. Stacks of flaky quiche, beautiful bowls of spinach salad, colorful miniature patisserie fruit tarts, and a simple iced cake, bring a still-life quality to the buffet table. "Placing like objects together, en masse, magnifies their visual impact. Everything takes on a specialness and looks more sophisticated," Suzanne notes. Good friends enjoying sumptuous food, paired with abundant glasses of Veuve Clicquot, in a chic space, translates in any language. "The people, the stories told, and the memories made are what make gatherings special."

SUZANNE'S STYLE NOTES

PRE-PARTY BASICS: *table set the day before*

BAR BASICS: *a silver tray*

MUST HAVE: *William Yeoward crystal*

LINENS: *Jenny Johnson Allen*

FAVORITE GIFT TO GIVE: *a signed copy of my book,* Sophisticated Simplicity

FAVORITE GIFT TO RECEIVE: *a bottle of Veuve Clicquot*

STAYING PARTY-READY: *linens cleaned and pressed*

FAVORITE BUBBLY: *a glass of Veuve Clicquot*

PARTY PET PEEVE: *late guests*

CANDLES: *always unscented*

FLOWERS: *roses and cherry blossom branches*

GUEST SOAP: *Savon de Marseille Extra Pur Coton*

SPINACH AND STRAWBERRY SALAD

Serves 4

Beautiful ripe strawberries, almond slivers, and rich green spinach, all tossed with sesame seed dressing, is pure perfection. Choose brightly colored, firm, plump strawberries for the salad. Look for berries with fresh green caps intact. Avoid soft, shriveled berries. Also, eschew strawberries that are partly white or unripe as they do not ripen after they are picked.

Strawberries are highly perishable. Most will keep for 2 or 3 days, but are best used within 24 hours of purchasing. If you are not using or consuming the berries on the day of purchase, spread them out on a shallow plate, cover with paper towels, and store in a sealed container or plastic bag in a cool place.

½ cup sugar
¼ cup apple cider vinegar
2 tablespoons sesame seeds
1 ½ teaspoons minced red onion
¼ teaspoon Worcestershire sauce
¼ teaspoon paprika
½ cup light olive oil
½ pound baby spinach
1 pint strawberries, hulled and quartered
¼ cup almond slivers, toasted

In a medium bowl, whisk together the sugar, vinegar, sesame seeds, onion, Worcestershire sauce, and paprika. Slowly whisk in the olive oil.

Place the spinach and strawberries in a salad bowl and toss with the dressing. Top with toasted almonds and serve.

SOUP
ON SUNDAY
Ronda Carman

Socialite Nan Kempner was famous for her Sunday night spaghetti buffets in New York City. She lived in the same sixteen-room duplex at 79th Street and Park Avenue for more than forty-five years and hosted hundreds of such dinners. An invitation to one of her Sunday shindigs was coveted. The hostess once said, "The secret to a good party is not lavish menus, place settings, and flowers, but imagination and great friends." Notably, some of her best parties were casual affairs with spaghetti.

After living in Scotland for several years, I implemented my own version of Nan's Sunday night spaghetti suppers. Scottish weather, more often than not, is wet, dark, and cold. The word Scots use to describe such weather is *dreich*—dull, dismal, and dreary. Most days I would draw the shades on daytime well before dinnertime. Having friends over for Sunday dinners gave me something to look forward to each week. Not to mention, it provided an opportunity to indulge my love of cooking. No matter how simple the setting, each dinner was a special occasion.

Despite my enjoyment of pasta, I find myself longing for soup on the stove and table. Soup has always been my true food love. It is the ultimate comfort food, and Sunday is the perfect day to slow down and enjoy its humble satisfaction. It soothes the soul, nourishes the unwell, and, in my case, unites friends on Sundays.

Now that I am back in my home state of Texas, I lean toward light broths and chilled soups most of the time, as cool days here are few and far between. However, the first nip in the air pulls me outside and puts me in search of a hearty soup recipe. Entertaining alfresco in this humid part of the world is a rare treat, and most often spontaneous. When the opportunity does come along, I remind myself that an enjoyable outdoor dinner party does not demand great planning or anything elaborate—just simple food, good company, and a welcoming location.

On chillier days I love to make chowders and fish stews. And, when it comes to seafood, I always engage my husband to help with the selection. Having grown up sailing the Gulf Coast and exploring all of its nooks and crannies, he is well versed in the subject and is especially knowledgeable about oysters. As a young child, his father would give oysters to clients every year for Christmas. He and his younger sister would happily accompany their dad to collect these delicacies, eating as many raw oysters as the amused boat crew would shuck for the little ones.

AN OYSTER PRIMER

Oysters are a lot like wine and reflect the flavor of their surroundings. When choosing oysters, rely on four of your senses.

SMELL: *Fresh oysters should smell crisp and briny, much like seawater. They should not smell fishy. Pre-shucked oysters should have no ammonia smell.*

SIGHT: *Look to see that the oysters are being kept on ice in a well-drained refrigerated case and that the shells are shut tight. You want a flat top and a deep cup (the bottom half). The deeper the cup, the more room for meat and brine.*

TOUCH: *Oyster shells are rough to the touch and may have barnacles. Toss oysters with excessive algae, seaweed, discoloration, or moss. These are signs of poor tank storage and water circulation.*

TASTE: *Ask to taste the oysters, if possible. As a general rule, the Atlantic produces oysters with a sharp brininess and an intense hit of the fresh, cold sea. Pacific oysters are rarely salty and often taste complex and sweet. The combination of fresh water and salt water from the Gulf of Mexico contributes to the unique taste of a Gulf Coast oyster; as a rule of thumb, they are larger and meatier than those from other coastal areas.*

OYSTER STEW

Serves 4 to 6

My go-to oyster stew is an adaption from two of my favorite men—my father-in-law, David Whitaker, and American restaurant critic, food journalist, cookbook author, and long-time food editor for the *New York Times* Craig Claiborne. Serve with classic oyster crackers as an accompaniment.

4 tablespoons unsalted butter
½ cup finely chopped yellow onion
½ cup finely chopped celery
3 tablespoons minced shallot
½ cup dry sherry
3 cups whole milk
1 cup half-and-half
2 teaspoons Worcestershire sauce
½ teaspoon Tabasco sauce
¼ teaspoon paprika
Salt and freshly ground black or
    white pepper to taste
1 pint shucked oysters, in their natural liquor
¼ cup finely chopped flat-leaf parsley

In a stockpot, melt the butter over medium-high heat. Add the onion, celery, and shallots. Cook until soft, 3 minutes.

Add the sherry and bring to a low simmer. Gently stir in the milk, half-and-half, Worcestershire sauce, Tabasco sauce, paprika, salt, and pepper. Bring to a low simmer.

Add the oysters with their liquor and simmer until the oysters start to curl, about 3 minutes. Do not overcook or the oysters will become tough. To serve, ladle the stew into heated soup bowls. Sprinkle with parsley, and serve with oyster crackers.

A BARBECUE
BIRTHDAY BASH
Denise and Scott McGaha

Weekend chef Scott McGaha is a grill master. His wife Denise, an interior designer, is a mix master. Together the two create meaningful and memorable parties. To celebrate the birthday of their sister-in-law, Teresa, the duo cooked up an unforgettable afternoon for family and friends. Making the occasion easy and enjoyable for the guest of honor, Denise and Scott brought the party to Teresa's backyard. The beautiful three-acre property on the outskirts of Dallas is a true refuge. A meandering creek hugs the edge of the lawn and large oak trees create uninterrupted canopies under which to dine.

As the sun comes up, Scott fires up the grill and Denise dresses the table. Woven antique baskets are used to transport everything needed for the day. A timber slab, covered with a fabric designed by Denise for Design Legacy, lays the base for a festive affair. The celeste cloth is topped with a mix of wooden chargers and vintage blue-and-white plates from Marché Paul Bert Serpette in Paris. White porcelain salad plates, a wedding gift from a dear friend, sit atop the stacks of dishes. Letterpress menus offer a preview of what is to come—tri-tip steak with chimichurri sauce, skillet chicken thighs with preserved lemon, butter-braised fingerling potatoes, and grilled heirloom carrots are all on offer.

Emerald-green glasses and clear stemware brimming with ruby-red wine and brioche-colored Champagne echo the colors of the flowers. Antique velvet dining chairs and a weather-worn teak sofa lined with mismatched pillows keep the vibe casual yet pulled-together. Knowing that barbecues, birthdays, and boozy beverages go hand in hand, Denise turns a corner of the yard into an alfresco bar. Monogrammed linens, rattan ice buckets, and novelty glassware add an extra-festive look. Bowls filled with lemons and limes double as decor.

Long before guests arrive, Scott turns on music to set the mood and begins prepping. It is an activity that he enjoys as much as grilling. Rhythmically chopping wood, dicing pungent herbs, and slicing luscious lemons is his preferred method of therapy. Even with an impressive repertoire of recipes, he usually selects tried-and-true favorites. "I always revert back to simple fare," the cook admits. "I think people like unpretentious foods made with really fresh ingredients." The first hint of smoke produces teasing aromas and calls everyone to the fire pit. To complete the celebratory lineup, Scott throws a pineapple on the grill—it will be used to create a Dutch oven cobbler. The barbecue birthday is the epitome of a casual, sophisticated celebration. From the epicurean menu to the well-dressed table, set simply yet beautifully, nothing is sacrificed for substance or style.

Backyard BBQ

Asadores Tri-tip with Chimichurri Sauce

Lemon Preserve Skillet Fried Chicken

Butter Braised Fingerling Potatoes

Heirloom Carrots

Dutch Oven Pineapple Cobbler with Crème Fraiche

SCOTT'S GRILLING TIPS

Scott grew up in Louisiana grilling with his dad and uncles. From hamburgers and venison to fresh seafood and other wild game, the family relished big dinners. Scott's favorite things to grill include pork tenderloin, tri-tip steak, and fresh vegetables. Here are some of his tried-and-true tips:

Start your fire early if using wood to fuel your grill. I prefer to not use a synthetic fire starter.

Have enough room in your fire to move the coals around for different cooking temperatures.

Do not be afraid to cook low and slow over coals. It is the best way to achieve maximum flavor.

Always marinate meats at least twenty-four hours prior to grilling.

Be open to trying new techniques for grilling. A Patagonian cross is great for roasting different cuts, like prime rib, over an open fire with hot embers.

A cast-iron skillet, or Dutch oven, never disappoints.

A fresh bunch of rosemary, used as a brush, is a flavorful way to baste your meat throughout the grilling process. Use kitchen twine to tie the herbs to the end of a wooden spoon.

LEMON PRESERVE SKILLET FRIED CHICKEN

Serves 4

The next time you want to elevate chicken, try this recipe. The subdued bite and firm texture of the preserved lemons enrich the flavor of the dish. Use only thighs for a crisp outside and moist and juicy inside.

1 ½ tablespoons extra-light olive oil
½ tablespoon butter
8 bone-in chicken thighs
Salt and freshly ground black pepper to taste
1 preserved lemon rind, cut into strips

Prepare a gas or charcoal grill. Pour the olive oil into a large, heavy skillet (cast-iron works well) and warm the oil on an area of the grill with medium heat. Then add butter. Season the chicken thighs with salt and pepper and add them to the skillet, skin side down. Cook without moving until the fat has rendered and the skin is crisp and deep golden brown, 20 to 30 minutes.

Move the skillet to an area of the grill with medium-low heat. Turn the thighs and stir the preserved lemon strips into the fat collected in the skillet. Continue cooking until the meat closest to the bone is cooked through and a meat thermometer inserted registers 165°F, about 15 additional minutes. Plate the chicken, pour the pan drippings and lemon strips over the thighs, and serve immediately.

PRESERVED LEMONS

Makes 1 ½ pints

Preserved lemons are an essential ingredient in some North African and Middle Eastern cuisines. The delicious pickled rind adds wonderful citrus, salty, and lemony flavors to many types of recipes. The rinds are also a great addition to grilled dishes, a charcuterie tray, or as a tasty treat on their own.

5 whole organic lemons
⅓ cup kosher salt
Freshly squeezed lemon juice to cover the lemons, if needed

Wash the lemons well and trim the ends. Cut the lemons into quarters but stop before cutting all the way through so that the quarters are attached at the bottom. Sprinkle 1 teaspoon salt on each lemon and rub salt between each lemon slice; set aside.

Using a clean 1 ½-pint canning jar with an air-tight lid, add 2 tablespoons of salt to cover the bottom of the jar. Place 1 lemon in the jar. Press down on the lemon to release its juices and cover with another 1 teaspoon salt. Repeat the process with the remaining lemons and salt. Finish by topping the lemons with 2 tablespoons salt. The lemons should be fully submerged in their juices. Add extra lemon juice to cover if needed.

Tightly cover the jar with the lid. Shake the jar a few times. Leave at room temperature for two days, shaking the jar each day. On the third day, place the jar in the refrigerator. The lemons should be fully pickled in two to three weeks. To use, remove the desired amount of lemon needed. Discard the flesh of the lemon and the white pith, leaving only the yellow rind. Use the rind as instructed in a recipe or eat it as a snack.

Note: Preserved lemons will keep up to one year in the refrigerator. Make certain that the lemons are always submerged in lemon juice.

CHOWDER IN THE ORANGERIE
Bettie Bearden Pardee

Summertime in Newport, Rhode Island, is pure magic. Sailboats, sunshine, and socializing abound. Legendary for its stately mansions, stunning seascapes, world-class sailing, tennis whites, and gracious entertaining, Newport is the epitome of old school elegance. It is also home to author, gardener, and famed hostess Bettie Bearden Pardee. "I adore this place," she confesses, "I am so blessed to live in this 379-year-old city by the sea."

Renowned for her garden, it is her favorite place to entertain—specifically, her orangerie. The stunning structure, in the middle of an expansive lawn, was a Christmas gift from her husband. While they were walking through the snow he pulled a beautiful rendering from his jacket. "It was tied with a red bow. An extravagant surprise, but oh, so welcome," she fondly recalls.

The former *Bon Appétit* contributing editor is never too busy for entertaining fellow garden aficionados and friends. When inspired to host an impromptu lunch, she followed the lead of the New York Yacht Club's Harbour Court in Newport. "They do a wonderful chowder bar. It's hearty, easy, and delicious. Of course it is New England clam chowder. Is there any other?" Bettie laughs.

While hardly a global dish and specifically American, New England clam chowder is nevertheless renowned in culinary circles for its deliciousness and simplicity. Novelist Herman Melville devoted an entire chapter to chowder in his famous book *Moby Dick*, "It was made of small juicy clams, scarcely bigger than hazel nuts, mixed with pounded ship biscuit, and salted pork cut up into little flakes; the whole enriched with butter, and plentifully seasoned with pepper and salt."

Cold bottles of rosé, pots of chowder, warm crockeries, and an array of toppings await everyone's arrival. Beautiful bowls filled with a wide selection of garnishes—chopped halibut, baby shrimp, sea scallops, clams, Portuguese sausage, bacon, potatoes, red pepper, leek, and chives—allow each guest to personalize lunch. Paying homage to the town, while keeping it simple, Bettie turns to The Black Pearl. A local New England institution since the 1920s, the restaurant offers its famed chowder in cans. "Even *Travel + Leisure* sings its praises," she smiles. Her approach is proof positive that entertaining can be both easy and elegant.

After lunch, guests walk the grounds and relax in the garden. Bettie's green parterre bench is always a conversation starter. It is an intriguing piece of furniture that looks like something straight out of *Alice in Wonderland*. Twenty years ago, while pheasant shooting in Ireland, she encountered an intriguing piece of garden furniture. "The Earl of Ross had a large bench with swooping flourishes that resembled the devil's pitchfork. I knew then that I needed one," she tells a guest. She came home and settled on a spot with a promise to herself that she would one day recreate such a seat. It is now the star of her garden and a favorite of all who come to visit.

TYPES OF CHOWDER

Chef Louis P. De Gouy, author of the 1949 cookbook The Soup Book, noted, "Clam chowder is one of those subjects, like politics and religion, that can never be discussed lightly. Bring it up even incidentally, and all the innumerable factions of the clambake regions raise their heads and begin to yammer."

NEW ENGLAND clam chowder is distinguished by the presence of a dairy base that gives the soup a non-translucent white color and a creamy texture. According to The Yankee Cook Book, the recipe calls for salt pork, onions, potatoes, milk, butter, and, of course, clams. Although individual recipes vary, milk or cream is always present.

RHODE ISLAND clam chowder is classically known for its absence of milk or cream. The rich clear broth is loaded with potatoes, bacon, and either cherrystone clams or quahogs, depending on what is fresh that day. Quahogs (pronounced coe-hogs) are large and distinguished by size. Too tough to eat raw, they become soft and juicy when chopped and used in chowders.

MANHATTAN clam chowder is recognized by its red color. Tomatoes are used in place of milk or cream. Meaty top-neck clams are the briny backbone of this chowder. Often it is chock-full of potatoes, celery, carrots, and herbs. The result is

a tasty, vegetable-forward chowder. There is little evidence linking the recipe to Manhattan.

LONG ISLAND clam chowder is a variant that is part New England-style and part Manhattan-style, making it a creamy tomato clam chowder. The name is a geographical pun, in reference to the fact that the location of Long Island, just like the recipe, is halfway between Manhattan and New England.

PAIRING WINE WITH NEW ENGLAND CLAM CHOWDER

A rich, oaky, high-alcohol chardonnay from California has both the body and the complexity to stand up to a rich, cream-based soup. The texture of Champagne also pairs well with the thick soup, as its acidity cuts through cream. For something different, try a chilled glass of manzanilla sherry. Manzanilla has great acidity and a salty trace. Its saline quality complements clams. Other options include sauvignon blanc, a medium-bodied chenin blanc, a citrusy Gavi, or a crisp rosé.

COME FOR COCKTAILS

SPRING
FLING
Julia Reed

No one embodies the exuberant spirit of Southern hospitality more than Julia Reed. A journalist, food writer, and lifestyle expert, Julia is also the consummate hostess. Born and raised in the Mississippi Delta, she grew up at her mother's knee, polishing silver, preparing for parties, and frequently attending social gatherings.

No matter the occasion, there is always a lavish yet lighthearted quality to Julia's celebrations. An accomplished cook, she does not shy away from foods that she loves or recipes that call for Pepperidge Farm Very Thin white bread, canned soup, or Uncle Ben's converted rice. And she will be the first to extol the virtues of serving Popeyes fried chicken alongside Champagne at dinner parties.

After selling her New Orleans Greek Revival house, made famous in her best-selling memoir, *The House on First Street*, Julia relocated to a nearby apartment in the Garden District. It is now a hub for frequent visitors from out of town and numerous festivities. Julia's favorite form of entertaining is not a seated dinner, but instead what she calls a "cocktail supper"—food passed on trays and spread out along the dining table, with enough fare to constitute a full meal. It allows her guests to mix, mingle, eat, and drink without worrying about using silverware or finding a place to rest a glass.

Even when Julia has only a couple of people over for a quick drink, there will be a signature concoction, a full bar, homemade cheese straws, roasted pecans, pickled okra, various dips, and an abundance of flowers. The hostess subscribes to the theory that more is more, but she does not overdo it on the flowers. She prefers masses of a single seasonal bloom in low cylindrical vases. "I've been to too many parties where the flowers are so heavy-handed it looks like somebody died," she laughs.

For her spring fling, Julia opts for daffodils and kumquats. The libation of choice is a Champagne cocktail with Fee Brothers grapefruit bitters served in nineteenth-century French Champagne flutes. Her affinity for mixing an interesting cast of characters extends beyond people. It is reflected in her home, serving pieces, and stemware. Antique wine goblets from Lucullus, on Chartres Street, mingle with over-sized monogrammed napkins, vintage china, silver cups, and Riedel glasses. "There is an extravagance about Southern get-togethers, but that doesn't mean they're excessive or overdone. It's more about graciousness and a desire to show your guests genuine warmth," she explains.

JULIA'S GRAPEFRUIT CHAMPAGNE COCKTAIL

Makes 4 cocktails

The celebratory Champagne cocktail is a simple yet sumptuous concoction. The traditional recipe calls for a mixture of bitters, bubbles, and a sugar cube. Julia opts for Fee Brothers grapefruit bitters rather than the customary Angostura bitters. Kumquats as a garnish impart a very distinctive taste. This is the only citrus fruit that can be eaten with the skin. Most agree that brut Champagne makes the best partner.

4 sugar cubes, preferably La Perruche
4 dashes Fee Brothers grapefruit bitters
1 bottle brut Champagne
4 kumquat slices

Soak each sugar cube in a dash of bitters and drop into a Champagne flute. Fill the four flutes with Champagne. Garnish each with a slice of kumquat.

MORE ABOUT BITTERS

Bitters are the key ingredient in the classic Champagne cocktail. Known as the salt and pepper of the cocktail world, bitters are made from botanicals such as aromatic herbs, bark, roots, and fruit. They add a layer of flavor to simple drinks. Likewise, they can balance sweet and sour flavors or impart complexity to stirred cocktails.

Bitters had their heyday in the 1800s before largely disappearing at the turn of the twentieth century, primarily due to governmental regulation. Prohibition was the final nail in the coffin for almost all brands. Some of the oldest bitters companies, Angostura, Fee Brothers, and Peychaud's, continue today and are regarded as among the best of the producers.

BAR BITES

Caviar with potato chips and crème fraîche
Cheese straws (in most of the South, they are a must)
Crab cakes
Crab dip
Deviled eggs
Garlic shrimp
Hot cheese olives
Peanuts
Pickled okra
Smoked oysters
Spicy pecans

BOURBON AND BOWTIES
Bill Ingram

Architect Bill Ingram is as passionate about parties as he is about historic homes, architecture, and period details. The Atlanta resident and veteran host knows how to marry traditional Southern charm with modern sensibilities.

Bill is celebrated for his dinner parties, but he equally loves a fun rousing cocktail party—especially before the theater. Throwing a pre-theater affair is a lot like directing. The timing is crucial and casting goes into the guest list. The food and drink menu is much like a dialogue; it moves everything forward. "Too much food can be a turn-off," the host cautions. "Moreover, what you serve needs to match the intensity and duration of the alcohol to avoid scathing reviews."

Keenly aware that guests will be standing or perched on chairs, Bill calls on caterer Dennis Dean for easy-to-eat options. An array of finger foods offers something for everyone—roast beef sliders, rosemary chicken skewers, bacon-wrapped pretzel rods, and pimento cheese with various types of vegetables and crackers. The portions should be generous enough to keep appetites at bay for the night. "Everything should be ready when guests arrive. This isn't the type of party that will unfold over the course of an evening," Bill notes.

A dramatic apricot dining room sets the tone for the evening. Guests are ushered into the room through a pair of high-gloss black doors, while sumptuous Fortuny fabric skirts tall windows. A round dining table, faux-bamboo chairs, and orange velvet cushions with tassels take center stage. Suspended from the soft blue grass-cloth ceiling, an over-scaled crystal chandelier with silk shades casts a soft glow.

Just off the dining room a full bar awaits. Tonight, bourbon is the crown jewel. A myriad of well-known and small-batch bottles stands at attention—Jefferson's, Knob Creek, Old Forester, Maker's Mark, Woodford Reserve, Elijah Craig. Strictly an American concoction, bourbon is drunk by Southerners with pleasure and abandon, much as the French drink wine. An affable, well-informed bartender pours and shares tasting notes on the different varieties—a gesture appreciated by guests. A firm believer that a small gathering benefits from having someone who will keep glasses filled, Bill often employs the help of one person. "It frees me to have fun and be a guest myself. If I am at ease, everyone else will be, too."

BILL ON BOURBON

AGING: *There are no age requirements for bourbon. To be called a straight bourbon, it must age for two years in new charred oak barrels. If aged for less than four years, the age must be stated on the bottle.*

ALCOHOL BY VOLUME: *Bourbon must be distilled to no more than 160 proof and bottled at no less than 80 proof.*

COLOR: *Light golden to rich amber.*

CONTENT: *Bourbon must contain at least 51 percent corn grain. More can be used, but anything less is whiskey, not bourbon.*

REGION: *Although associated with Kentucky, it can be crafted anywhere in the United States.*

POPULAR BOURBON-BASED COCKTAILS

Boulevardier	*Milk punch*
Brown derby	*Mint julep*
Hot toddy	*New York sour*
Manhattan	*Old fashioned*

BOURBON OLD-FASHIONED

Serves 1

1 sugar cube, preferably La Perruche French White
2 dashes Angostura bitters
2 ounces (¼ cup) bourbon
1 orange wedge
1 fresh cherry

Muddle the sugar cube and bitters with 1 teaspoon water at the bottom of a chilled rocks glass. Add the bourbon and stir.

Add 1 large ice cube. Stir until chilled and slightly diluted, about 30 seconds. Garnish with an orange wedge and a fresh cherry.

BACON-WRAPPED PRETZELS

Makes 14

Just a few simple ingredients join together in a salty-sweet masterpiece. Sugary, savory, and a little spicy, warm bacon wrapped around a pretzel rod is pure bliss.

14 slices (one 12-ounce package) thin sliced bacon, preferably Oscar Mayer Original Center Cut Hardwood Smoked Hand-Trimmed Bacon
1 cup packed brown sugar
3 tablespoons chili powder
1/8 teaspoon cayenne pepper
Sea salt to taste
14 pretzel rods

Preheat the oven to 375°F. Line a baking sheet with parchment. Place a wire rack on top of the lined baking sheet. Allow the bacon to sit at room temperature for 5 minutes.

Mix the brown sugar, chili powder, and cayenne pepper in a small bowl. Season to taste with salt.

Spread the brown sugar mix onto a large flat dish. Dredge both sides of each bacon slice in the brown sugar mixture.

Wrap a coated bacon slice around the entire length of each pretzel rod. Arrange the wrapped pretzels on the wire rack on top of the baking sheet. Bake until the bacon is crisp, 15 to 20 minutes. Let cool on the wire rack for 20 minutes, then serve.

Note: When the pretzels come out of the oven, they will be limp and soft to touch. The pretzels will harden as they cool. Do not place pretzels on a paper towel as they will stick.

SOUTHERN PIMENTO CHEESE

Makes 3 ½ cups

Serve with biscuits, crackers, pita chips, toasted baguettes, deviled eggs, apple slices, sliced carrots, celery, and bell peppers.

2 cups shredded extra-sharp cheddar cheese
8 ounces cream cheese, softened
½ cup mayonnaise, preferably Hellmann's or Duke's
1 ½ teaspoons Worcestershire sauce
1 ½ teaspoons dry mustard
¼ teaspoon garlic powder
¼ teaspoon ground cayenne pepper
¼ teaspoon onion powder
One 4-ounce jar diced pimentos, drained
Salt and freshly ground black pepper to taste

Place the cheddar cheese, cream cheese, mayonnaise, Worcestershire, dry mustard, garlic powder, cayenne, onion powder, and the pimentos into the large bowl of a mixer fitted with a paddle attachment. Beat at medium-low speed until well mixed. Season with salt and black pepper.

Cover the bowl with plastic wrap and refrigerate for 8 to 12 hours. When ready to serve, let the mixture stand at room temperature for 30 minutes. Stir well before serving.

PIMENTO CHEESE PRIMER

To the uninitiated, pimento cheese is little more than grated cheese, diced pimento peppers, and mayonnaise. To devotees, pimento cheese is a must-have food favorite that elevates an ordinary sandwich into something blissful. The popularity of this unique spread remains largely confined to states below the Mason-Dixon line. It is hard to believe that this Southern delicacy actually got its start in New York.

CHEESE: Enthusiasts agree that extra-sharp cheddar cheese is a must for this beloved recipe—its sharpness is the backbone. Stick with yellow cheddar to maintain pimento cheese's signature color.

MAYONNAISE: High-quality mayonnaise is a given. Real mayonnaise is a must. Hellmann's and Duke's are Southern favorites.

COCKTAILS IN THE KITCHEN
Shelly Rosenberg

When you arrive at the Dallas home of Shelly Rosenberg, you know immediately that you are in for a special evening. A colossal portrait by Spanish artist Alberto Gálvez greets guests before they even make their way through the front door. The oil painting's translucent glazes of color on linen create an ethereal glow. In the dining room, graceful dancing flames glimmer in an elongated fireplace. A sweeping wall of endless glass blurs the lines between the indoors and outside. The vibe is reminiscent of Philip Johnson's Glass House, a modernist masterpiece in New Canaan, Connecticut. And just as Philip and his partner, David Whitney, would invite great minds for an evening of discussion, drinks, and dialogue, Shelly and her husband, Barry, do the same.

A mother of three and frequent hostess, Shelly knows all too well that the best parties seem to start and end in the kitchen. When envisioning their dream house, the couple opted for an open, refined, and relaxing respite conducive to entertaining. She relied on her design background to realize their vision of a family-friendly, cozy, contemporary home. Each room seamlessly opens onto the next. The modish kitchen blends easily with the living area, and appliances are disguised behind refined wooden panels. The result is an urbane and sophisticated space. Rich, saturated hues of brown, olive, gold, and ivory, blend with walnut wood, luminous brass, and matte black finishes. The effect is both contemporary and elegant. "We wanted a place that feels modern, but not so right-this-minute that it's going to be dated in a few years."

To christen their new home, the couple invited friends over for cocktails in the kitchen. Looking for a novel angle to capture the tastes of the season, Shelly turned to Cynthia Mulcahy of Mulcahy Farms. Known for herbs and edible flowers, the farm supplies the best bars and restaurants in the city. When presented with a grand mix of violets and pansies, Shelly got the idea to freeze the gorgeous petals into ice molds that are traditionally used for serving scotch on the rocks. The two-inch spherical orbs are simultaneously refreshing and impressive. Imparting a slightly grassy and minty flavor, pansies partner perfectly with vodka and cocktails. To surprise her guests, the hostess created a frothy vodka sour to pair with the petals. As the foam dissipates, stunning floral ice balls are revealed.

Vases of chervil, lavender, lemon verbena, and spearmint double as decorative arrangements and delectable garnishes, while also scenting the kitchen. Deviled eggs are topped with appetizing flowers, marcona almonds are sprinkled with rosemary, fresh honeycomb is paired with herbed brie, and tiny basil leaves are sandwiched between blackberries and buffalo mozzarella. The evening is an engaging, visual, and palatable occasion that engrosses all of the senses.

MUST-HAVE BAR TOOLS

BAR SPOON: *Bartenders use this practical instrument to stir, measure, layer, and muddle cocktail ingredients. Made of stainless steel, it is durable and easy to clean.*

BOTTLE OPENER: *Before enjoying your favorite bottle of wine or beer, you need to open it. Waiters and sommeliers have long favored the corkscrew wine opener. With a sturdy two-hinge lever, it creates ideal leverage for bottle opening without breaking the cork. Flat openers, or bar keys, are a must-have staple for removing bottle caps with ease. The well-equipped bar has a range of openers.*

HAWTHORNE STRAINER: *Composed of a disk with stabilizing prongs and a metal spring, this important accessory is used to separate ice and other solid ingredients while pouring cocktails into a glass.*

JIGGER: *This hourglass-shaped measuring device ensures accurate amounts of alcohol for every drink.*

MUDDLER: *An essential bartender's tool, a muddler is used to mix and mash (or muddle) fruits, herbs, and spices in the bottom of a glass to extract essential oils. It is a necessity for crafting some of the most popular cocktails, including the caipirinha, mojito, and old-fashioned.*

PARING KNIFE: *When it comes to cocktails and barware, so often we think liquid. Prepping garnishes is important, too. This little blade for slicing lemons, apples, and other garnishes should be part of every bar collection.*

SHAKER: *Used to mix and chill ingredients thoroughly, a shaker is the best tool for meticulously integrating flavors. The result is a cold concoction that is perfectly blended.*

USING EDIBLE FLOWERS

Always purchase edible flowers from the produce section of the grocery store or source them from a reliable farm. Avoid those that have been sprayed with pesticides or other chemicals.

Clean flowers by washing gently in a large bowl of cold water. Let the flowers air dry on a paper towels, then use immediately. If any are left over, store them in the refrigerator for up to 1 week in an airtight container lined with a damp paper towel.

VODKA SOUR

Serves 1

Most people think of whiskey as the traditional spirit in a sour cocktail. The same ingredients combine brilliantly with vodka. Egg whites add freshness and body, creating a refreshing drink. Angostura bitters bring complexity to an otherwise simple cocktail.

2 ounces (¼ cup) vodka, preferably Tito's
    or Zodiac
1 ounce (2 tablespoons) freshly squeezed
    lemon juice
½ ounce (1 tablespoon) simple syrup,
    such as Stirrings
3 dashes Angostura bitters
½ ounce (1 tablespoon) pasteurized egg whites
¾ cup crushed ice
1 floral ice sphere

Combine all ingredients, except the ice sphere, in a cocktail shaker. Place the large ice sphere in an old-fashioned glass. Shake the cocktail well and strain into the glass. Serve immediately.

A CHIC AND SIMPLE SOIRÉE
Caroline Harper Knapp

L ifestyle blogger Caroline Harper Knapp knows how to make magic happen. Even with a busy business and a popular blog, the mother of two little boys can pull together a party in a flash. Her blog, *House of Harper*, has become a lifestyle destination for foodies, fashionistas, and the design obsessed. It is a place where she shares advice, recipes, resources, and personal stories.

Caroline readily acknowledges that it can be hard at times to sit down for a meal, let alone prepare dinner for guests. Nevertheless, a helter-skelter schedule does not keep her from indulging her love of entertaining. Cocktail parties are some of her favorite gatherings. They are festive and glamorous, yet relatively stress-free. The light, airy, and stylish Houston home that she shares with her husband, Fred, is the ideal location for such occasions.

Their warm and welcoming entryway opens to a formal dining room and living area that offers several seating options. It is the perfect place to greet guests and pass drinks as everyone arrives. A signature tipple and a delicious cheese platter are musts in the Knapp house. They are simple touches that instantly make friends feel welcome while providing a little substance. Tonight the house drink is an Aperol spritz with lime. Low in alcohol, the gorgeous coral-colored cocktail pairs perfectly with prosecco.

Gold is Caroline's go-to party color. Incorporating the metallic hue makes everything feel like a celebration. Golden buckets filled with ice adorn several of the drink stations. Each of the bars is set up to allow guests to help themselves after the initial aperitif. Flatware, plates, glassware, bowls, candlelit sconces, and vases all gleam. Geometric shapes and patterns lend playfulness to the evening, while crisp white linens balance out the shine.

Beautiful charcuterie boards resembling still lifes adorn the dining table. Prosciutto, pistachios, olives, fresh vegetables, cheese, cheese straws, crackers, and dried and fresh fruit, including figs, apricots, and grapes, are all in the lineup. Not only is the prep simple, but the setup allows guests to eat and hold their drinks at the same time, making it easy to catch up with friends.

When it comes to tabletop decor Caroline relishes the unexpected. "I'm always looking for ways to adorn the table with something other than just flowers," she acknowledges. Whether in the form of hand-dipped beeswax candles, purple artichokes tied with twine, or large slabs of marble embracing the food, rich colors and interesting textures top her list of elements for creating a memorable affair.

APEROL SPRITZ

Serves 1

Aperol is an Italian aperitif made of gentian, rhubarb, and cinchona. The traditional Aperol spritz recipe calls for prosecco and orange slices. In Venice, it is often made with dry white wine and accompanied by a salty green olive. For this version, Caroline uses limes in place of oranges.

4 ½ ounces (generous ½ cup) brut prosecco, such as Mionetto
2 ½ ounces (⅓ cup) Aperol
1 lime wedge
1 ounce (2 tablespoons) club soda
2 or 3 fresh mint leaves

Pour the prosecco into a Collins glass filled with ice. Add the Aperol and lime wedge. Top with club soda, garnish with mint leaves, and serve.

CHARCUTERIE BOARD

Dione Lucas, the first female graduate of Le Cordon Bleu, noted, "The preparation of good food is merely another expression of art, one of the joys of civilized living." Here are Caroline's suggestions for an artistic and imaginative charcuterie board.

PURPLE GREEK ALPHONSO OLIVES: *Large, purple olives with a fleshy texture and a full, ripe-olive flavor. A touch of sourness results from curing in red wine and red wine vinegar.*

SILANO GRILLED ARTICHOKE STEMS: *The stem is one of the most overlooked delicacies. Marinated in sunflower oil with herbs and spices, these stems are not only tender and delicious but are also full of antioxidants.*

PIPARRAS PEPPERS: *These slender peppers have the perfect balance of a pickled flavor with a slight punch of heat. This traditional Basque pepper pairs perfectly with olives, anchovies, and manchego cheese.*

BLEU MONT BANDAGE-WRAPPED CHEDDAR: *A unique cheddar crafted in Blue Mounds, Wisconsin. The cheese is made in a cave to maintain proper temperature and humidity. It is prepared in the traditional English style, using a muslin cloth wrapped around the exterior to preserve moisture.*

MOUSSE DU PÉRIGORD PÂTÉ: *Duck, chicken, truffles, and sherry are blended into pâté perfection. Handmade in small craft batches of all-natural ingredients, this pâté has had such notable fans as Craig Claiborne, Mimi Sheraton, and James Beard.*

OLIVIERS & CO OLIVE CHUTNEY WITH CANDIED LEMON: *Black olives, green olives, honey, candied lemon, and sage come together in this exquisite chutney, the perfect accompaniment to all types of cheeses.*

ONLINE SPECIALTY FOOD SOURCES

Artisan Specialty Foods	*La Tienda*
Browne Trading Company	*Market Hall Foods*
D'Artagnan	*MOUTH*
Dean & DeLuca	*Murray's Cheese*
Di Bruno Bros.	*OliveNation*
Elite Gourmet	*Oliviers & Co*
Food52	*Stonewall Kitchen*
Formaggio Kitchen	*Sur La Table*
Fromagination	*Williams Sonoma*
Gustiamo	*Zabar's*
iGourmet	*Zingerman's*
La Quercia	

SPIRITED SUPPERS

A RAINY
SUNDAY SUPPER
Pam Kelley

If you don't like the weather in Texas, wait five minutes and it will change. Anyone who has ever lived in the Lone Star State knows that the long-standing cliché is no exaggeration. In the time it takes to uncork a bottle of wine, black clouds and torrential rain can suddenly appear on the horizon.

Fortunately for friends of Pam Kelley, Mother Nature is no match for the veteran hostess. When weekend thunderstorms threaten her long-planned outdoor dinner party, she quickly clears the living room and sets up a large round table in front of a roaring fire. As if by design, Chippendale chairs, soft pillows, and a wall of windows offer guests a front-row seat to the spectacular storm just beyond French doors.

A jewel-toned linen tablecloth, fabricated from Schumacher's classics collection, anchors the space, revealing more of what is to come—a cheerful and cozy evening. Originally designed in 1918, the fresh, fun, colorful pattern presents the perfect palette for creating a memorable tabletop. A cast of characters trims the table. Flowering oregano, brown and green majolica pots, rattan chargers, pale purple stemware, English ironstone—each plays a supporting role.

For Pam, having friends around the table is more than just an opportunity to pull out all of the creative stops. It is a time to slow down and regenerate, and also a great excuse to putter in the kitchen. Known for designing inviting interiors, she approaches entertaining and cooking with the same fervor. "A casual weekend dinner is ideal for gathering company and jovial conversation."

French 75 cocktails and a glowing hearth offer visitors a welcome respite on a damp fall night, while fresh oysters and Veuve Clicquot lure others into the kitchen. Cioppino simmers on the stove, scenting the air. The rustic Italian-American fish stew is the preferred house dish. "I love this tried-and-true recipe," Pam shares. "It's a family favorite and perfect for a dark, rainy day."

Ruby red bottles of Antinori Villa Toscana wine and piping hot crockeries of stew beckon guests to the table. On a gloomy night, bright red tomatoes nestled under mussels in a vintage hotel silver tureen are rays of sunshine. Generous stacks of crusty slices of ciabatta bread stand at the ready, begging to soak up every last drop of the anchovy-infused broth. Oversized linen napkins offer everyone beautiful protection from dipping and dripping. "No one likes wimpy napkins," Pam laughs.

CIOPPINO

Serves 6

The name "cioppino" comes from *ciuppin*, a classic soup from the Liguria region of Italy. Similar in flavor to cioppino, *ciuppin* uses Mediterranean seafood and fewer tomatoes. In the late 1800s, cioppino became a staple of Italian immigrants who settled in the North Beach neighborhood of San Francisco. When a fisherman came home empty-handed, he would walk around with a pot asking other fishermen to chip in whatever they could spare. Anything that ended up in the pot became cioppino. Serve with plenty of crusty bread.

¼ cup extra-virgin olive oil
2 or 3 anchovy fillets, drained
1 teaspoon crushed red pepper flakes
4 or 5 cloves garlic, crushed
2 celery ribs, chopped
1 medium yellow onion, chopped
1 cup good-quality dry white wine
5 cups chicken stock

One 28-ounce can peeled tomatoes, preferably Cento Chef's Cut
Leaves of 4 sprigs fresh thyme
¼ cup flat-leaf parsley, chopped
1 pound mussels, scrubbed and debearded
1 ½ pounds halibut fillets, cut into 2-inch chunks
1 pound large shrimp, peeled and deveined
12 scallops, preferably a mix of bay and sea
Salt and freshly ground black pepper to taste

Heat the olive oil in a large pot on moderate heat for 2 to 3 minutes. Add the anchovies, allowing them to melt into the olive oil. Add the crushed red pepper and garlic and sauté for 1 minute.

Add the celery and onion and cook, stirring frequently, until they soften, at least 5 minutes, then add the wine. Bring to a boil; simmer until the wine is reduced by half, 5 to 6 minutes. Add the chicken stock, tomatoes, thyme, and parsley. Cover and simmer for 30 minutes.

Add the mussels to the cooking liquid. Cover and cook until the mussels begin to open, about 5 minutes. Add the halibut fillets, shrimp, and scallops. Simmer gently until the fish is just cooked through, stirring gently. Discard any mussels that do not open. Season with salt and pepper to taste. Ladle into warm bowls and serve immediately.

CIOPPINO AND WINE PAIRINGS

Cioppino pairs well with Sangiovese. Sangiovese is the dominant grape in Italy's Chianti wines. This grape is known for its vibrant acidity and substantial tannins, along with fresh cherry fruit and herbal scents. It is also a great complement to any dish with cooked tomatoes.

Due to the acidic tomatoes in this dish, it also pairs well with a Pinot Noir, Riesling, or a white Bordeaux.

Alternatively, try a Barbera. From Northern Italy, Barbera has been around longer than Cabernet Sauvignon, by nearly 1,000 years. This Italian grape, with its bright-red cherry character, stokes up the herb-infused broth.

A FIRESIDE FÊTE
Heather Chadduck Hillegas

For eight years Heather Chadduck Hillegas and her husband, David, would walk by the 100-year-old clapboard colonial house they now call home. Sitting high atop a hill, the sprawling Birmingham estate embodied the charm and privacy they both desired. When the couple spotted a For Sale sign in the yard, they quickly submitted an offer. Additionally, the duo sent a handwritten note to the owners of sixty-seven years. Included in the letter was a promise to restore and respect the magnificent home and property.

Once they had taken ownership, Heather, an interior decorator, turned her attention to the gardens and porches. "A porch is very important in the South. We are so fortunate that the climate allows us to sit outside for most of the year," she says with a smile. With a little work and restoration, both the front and back verandas were reestablished as functioning open-air rooms.

The rear terrace was in great disrepair, as were several other structures. Antique bricks found scattered around the acreage were set in a herringbone pattern, laying the foundation for the alfresco dining area. Original whitewashed stones from cracked and uneven sidewalks were repurposed to construct a large fireplace. Just off the kitchen, and accessible through a Dutch door, it is an ideal spot for entertaining small groups.

The Alabama abode is good-naturedly referred to as the Pineapple House. The tropical fruit has long symbolized hospitality and all the intangibles guests appreciate—warmth, welcome, and friendship. The pineapple connection started with gifts from family and friends referencing the couple's wedding at the Jamaican resort Round Hill, which also boasts a pineapple as its insignia. From doorknockers to napkins, the playful symbol now abounds.

On a cool afternoon, Heather, David, and their two German shorthaired pointers, Harley and Eloise, causally putter around the porch awaiting the arrival of friends for a supper by the hearth. Heather adorns the table with Vista Alegre dinnerware. The bold navy plates and graphic diagonal lines seamlessly mix with her more traditional pieces.

For autumnal blooms the hostess called on her friend Kathleen Varner, a floral designer and stylist. The pair selected a mix of roses and locally grown dahlias. The rich hues, with greenery foraged from the garden, are grouped in vintage blue-and-white export pottery and placed around the table. Warming spirits and an oversized antique cutting board filled with various cheeses, fruits, nuts, and fresh breads stave off appetites. Just before sunset, David throws more logs on the fire and Heather serves chicken potpies—the ultimate comfort food.

PLAYING FAVORITES

BOURBON: *Bulleit 95 rye whiskey*

CANDLE: *Diptyque Figuier*

CHAMPAGNE: *Veuve Clicquot and Henriot*

CHINA: *Herend fish scale and Anna Weatherley*

COLLECTION: *vintage white ironstone*

COOKBOOK: *Avec Eric by Eric Ripert*

DINNERWARE: *Pillivuyt French bistro china (it can go right into the dishwasher)*

FABRIC: *ticking stripe—it goes with everything*

FLATWARE: *vintage bamboo*

FLOWERS: *roses, peonies, and hydrangea from the garden—dahlias in the fall*

GLASSWARE: *anything stemless*

GUEST SOAP: *Aēsop*

HERBS: *basil for taste and sage for garnish*

LINENS: *Peacock Alley. My friends own the company and they can make anything.*

MUSTARD: *Maille*

NAPKINS: *inky blue linens or indigo block prints*

PARTY-READY PANTRY: *marcona almonds, Castelvetrano olives, and Southern cheese straws*

SCENT: *piñon wood to add to an outdoor fire*

SERVINGWARE: *old weathered cutting boards from around the world*

ZESTY CHICKEN POTPIE

Serves 4

Chicken potpie is the epitome of comfort food. The only thing required to make a potpie from scratch is a little patience. You can save yourself some time by purchasing a rotisserie chicken. Heather's version is a most satisfying dish on a crisp fall evening. For a bit of heat, she adds tomatoes with green chilies.

CRUST
1 ¼ cups all-purpose flour
1 stick (8 tablespoons) unsalted butter, cut into cubes
¼ teaspoon kosher salt
3 or 4 tablespoons cold water

FILLING
3 tablespoons extra-virgin olive oil
1 large shallot, chopped
2 cloves garlic, minced
2 large carrots, roughly chopped
½ teaspoon sea salt
¼ teaspoon freshly ground black pepper
½ teaspoon minced fresh thyme leaves
3 tablespoons all-purpose flour
1 ½ cups chicken stock
2 cups shredded cooked chicken
1 cup frozen peas, thawed
One 10-ounce can diced tomatoes with green chilies, drained
1 large egg, lightly beaten

FOR THE CRUST: In a bowl, blend together the flour, the butter, and the kosher salt. With your fingertips, or a pastry blender, blend until the butter is combined with the flour and forms pea-size lumps. Using a fork, stir in 3 tablespoons water. Squeeze a handful of the dough. If it is still crumbly, stir in the remaining 1 tablespoon water. Gather the dough into a ball, then form it into a disk and wrap in plastic wrap. Chill the dough in the refrigerator for at least 1 hour.

Place the dough on a floured work surface. Using a floured rolling pin, roll the dough into a 10-inch disk. Cut four 4-inch rounds from the dough with a circular cutter. You can create decorative medallions with the scraps. Refrigerate

the cut dough until ready to use. Meanwhile, preheat the oven to 400°F.

FOR THE FILLING: In a large skillet, heat the oil over medium-high heat until hot. Stir in the shallot, garlic, carrots, sea salt, black pepper, and thyme. Cook, stirring occasionally, 8 to 10 minutes. Stir in the flour and cook until incorporated, about 2 minutes. Slowly pour in the stock, stirring as you do, and bring to a low boil. Once the mixture starts to thicken, stir in the chicken, peas, and tomatoes. Cook until the mixture is thick and well combined, about 5 minutes. Taste and adjust the seasoning.

Divide the filling among four 8-ounce ramekins. Place one pastry round over the top of each ramekin. Press the crust gently against the inside of each ramekin to seal. Brush the top of each potpie with the beaten egg. Arrange any decorations on top and brush again. Cut a small slit in the top of the pastry to create a steam vent. Place the ramekins on a baking sheet. Bake the potpies until the filling is bubbling and the pastry is golden, 20 to 25 minutes.

PEAR AND DIJON BAKED BRIE

Serves 6

Honey, walnuts, fresh sage, and a jar of Maille old-style whole grain Dijon mustard are staples Heather keeps on hand. These ingredients can easily transform any dish. This recipe is a delicious adaptation created by the Runway Chef for Maille. Serve with toasted baguette slices or crackers and extra mustard.

One 9 ½-ounce wheel Brie
2 tablespoons Maille whole grain Dijon mustard
1 pear, thinly sliced
1 tablespoon chopped walnuts
1 ½ teaspoons honey

Preheat the oven to 350°F. Line a baking sheet with parchment paper and place the Brie in the center. Spread the mustard on top, then arrange the pear slices decoratively in a single layer on top of the mustard and sprinkle with the walnuts.

Bake just until the cheese starts to melt, 5 to 7 minutes. Drizzle with honey and serve immediately.

A HEARTY HARVEST SUPPER

Ruth Davis

Ruth Davis is a natural-born hostess. Hospitality is in her blood. In rural Mississippi, where she grew up, there were no restaurants and no country clubs, so everyone entertained at home. "My parents always extended last-minute invitations for steaks and baked potatoes. It was casual and low-key," she recalls. Her mother, grandmothers, and aunts were all great cooks—the food was simple, straightforward, and sublime. No gimmicks. No nonsense. Flavors were always fresh and seasonal. Those are the same principles Ruth employs today for her hearty harvest supper.

When fall finally returns to the South, you can almost hear a collective sigh of relief. Just a hint of cool air grants Southern dwellers a welcome reprieve. Simply knowing that you have survived another hot August is reason enough to rejoice and celebrate. And while September may officially mark the end of summer, often a calendar is your only clue that cooler days are coming. To commemorate the approaching season, Ruth and her husband, Neill, turn their enviable study into an intimate dining room. As the autumn sun tracks low across the sky, a soft golden hue replaces the familiar summertime glare. The abundance of autumnal light floods the cozy space. A wall of tall windows lets falling leaves cast their shadows on polished concrete floors and high-gloss laminate walls. An Eero Saarinen table, used as a desk, becomes a dining table once again.

The library-cum-dining room offers guests the kind of stylish setting for which the Davises are known. Though the space is beautifully appointed, good old-fashioned warmth abounds. When the couple designed their home they opted for comfortable and livable rooms, with flexibility for entertaining. Ruth, co-owner of FOUND, an influential home design boutique, is known not only for her entertaining prowess, but also for mixing period antiques and repurposing modern finds to create unassuming decor.

Her aesthetic leans toward minimalism and she is no fan of fussy fare. For this early October celebration, the hostess opts for a pared-down tabletop. Custom crocheted linen napkins serve dual duty by also gently cradling handwritten place cards. Brass cutlery, pin candlesticks, cut vines from the backyard, wooden chargers, and simple white plates provide a flawless backdrop for rustic duck confit, fresh figs, winter squash cakes, braised Swiss chard, and wild rice.

For dessert, guests are treated to miniature lemon tarts topped with the last of the fresh berries. It is a final reminder of summer's departure, and a promise that it will come around again next year.

STAYING STOCKED
RUTH RECOMMENDS

A good supply of tea light candles and a long-handled lighter

A large supply of Williams Sonoma hotel dinner napkins, ironed and ready to go

A wide selection of white dinnerware, including serving bowls and platters

Buy more dinner plates than you think you need.

You can never have too many wine and Champagne glasses.

A variety of vases in various sizes

CB2, Canvas Home, and West Elm are wonderful sources for inexpensive tabletop accessories.

Food52 is a great aggregator of unique items for the kitchen made by artisans.

My main go-to source is my home store, FOUND. We always have fun finds for the table.

SIMPLE DUCK CONFIT

Serves 8

Making confit is a time-tested French technique for preserving duck legs in fat. Although most people no longer need to keep duck through the winter without refrigeration, the technique is still used today because it imparts delicious flavor. Serve the duck over wild rice.

1 ½ teaspoons kosher salt
1 teaspoon freshly ground black pepper
2 bay leaves, crumbled
3 sprigs thyme, leaves stripped from stems
1 sprig rosemary, leaves stripped from stem
8 Moulard duck legs, rinsed and patted dry
   (do not trim)

In a small bowl, combine the salt, pepper, bay leaf pieces, thyme, and rosemary. Sprinkle the duck legs generously with the mixture. Place the duck legs in a single layer in a roasting pan or other container large enough to hold them in a single layer. Cover tightly with plastic wrap and refrigerate for 24 hours.

The following day, preheat the oven to 325°F. Place the duck legs, fat side down, in a large ovenproof skillet. Arrange the legs in a snug single layer (if necessary, use two skillets to avoid overcrowding).

Heat the duck legs on the stove over medium-high heat until the duck starts to render its fat. Once there is 1/4 inch of rendered fat in the skillet(s), about 20 minutes, gently flip the duck legs. Carefully cover the skillet(s) with foil and place them in the preheated oven.

Roast the legs for 2 ½ hours. Remove the foil and continue roasting until duck is golden brown, about 1 additional hour. Remove the duck from its fat and serve.

Note: This method of preparing duck is truly simple and outrageously good. The cooked duck legs will last for five days in the refrigerator. When ready to serve, reheat in a 350°F oven until warm. Once warmed through, place the legs under the broiler until crisp.

AN EASY SATURDAY SUPPER
Cathy Kincaid

Interior designer Cathy Kincaid is known for skillfully mixing modern art with bold patterns and timeless antiques. As with design, she fashions colorful celebrations and casual dinners that foster a sense of elegance and ease. "My parties are unassuming and low-key," declares Cathy. Whether guests are sipping cocktails, listening to music, or watching sports, the hostess prefers that they join her in the kitchen.

Cathy's easygoing attitude is on full display this sunny Saturday afternoon. Before a game of tennis, she sets the table with elegantly embroidered Constance Leiter linens, blue-and-red Ceralene china, and etched crystal glasses. Bowls of ruby red cherries, pink peonies, and scarlet-colored soup complement the colors of the table. Each small detail makes the casual meal feel like an event. After a leisurely lunch with friends, Cathy stops by the bakery for tomato tarts that will accompany bowls of spicy gazpacho, and crispy breadsticks for the supper. "I love comfort food. Nothing fancy," she confesses.

Her love of comfort is also evidenced in her 1940s shingled New England–style home in Dallas. Each room radiates a spirit of coziness and exudes the charm of a country cottage. It is clearly a place where people live and every room is loved. Antiques, period pieces, and aged objects lend an air of warmth, novelty, and history. It all comes together to create interest and evoke a sense of comfortable elegance. "All of my rooms have evolved over time. I love to collect and I am always filtering my preferences," she notes.

The dining room, just large enough to accommodate a French Restoration table and early nineteenth-century Directoire chairs, makes the space feel even more cozy. Do not let the art, Staffordshire porcelain, or fine objects fool you. Despite hand-painted walls and stately antiques, nothing feels off-limits, not even to her four-legged friends. Before guests arrive, Otis (a soft wheaten terrier), Lilibet (a golden doodle), India (a cockapoo), and Queenie (a Norwich terrier) sneak into the dining room to take a nap by the fire.

As with all gatherings she assembles, this evening is no different. Tonight, Cathy has one clear goal in mind—an easy and intimate dinner by the fire with friends. "I love to entertain and I love my home. This is where I really enjoy sharing time with my family and friends."

EASY SPICY GAZPACHO

Serves 4

Gazpacho, a refreshing cold soup made of raw, blended vegetables, is widely eaten in Spain and Portugal, particularly during the hot summers. Loaded with tomatoes, cucumbers, red onion, garlic, and bell pepper, the unassuming soup originated in the southern Spanish region of Andalusia. This version takes a Texas detour with the use of spicy tomato juice. To omit the heat, use a mild tomato juice.

1 ½ pounds vine-ripened tomatoes
1 ½ cups spicy tomato juice, preferably
   Dei Fratelli Tasty Tom
1 cucumber, peeled, seeded, and chopped
½ cup chopped red bell pepper
½ cup chopped yellow bell pepper
½ cup chopped red onion
1 small Anaheim pepper, seeded and minced
2 small cloves garlic, minced
¼ cup extra-virgin olive oil
Freshly squeezed juice of 1 lime
2 teaspoons sherry vinegar
2 ½ teaspoons Worcestershire sauce
½ teaspoon ground cumin
1 teaspoon kosher salt
¼ teaspoon freshly ground black pepper
¼ cup tightly packed basil leaves, for garnish
Chopped cherry tomatoes, for garnish

Fill a 6-quart pot halfway with water. Set the pot over high heat and bring to a boil. Fill a large bowl with ice water.

Make an X with a paring knife on the bottom of each tomato. Drop the tomatoes into the boiling water for 15 seconds, then remove with a slotted spoon and transfer to the bowl of ice water.

Allow the tomatoes to cool enough to handle, approximately 1 minute. Remove the tomatoes from the ice bath and pat dry. Peel, core, seed, and chop the tomatoes.

Place the tomatoes and juice in a large mixing bowl. Add the cucumber, bell peppers, red onion, Anaheim pepper, garlic, olive oil, lime juice, sherry vinegar, Worcestershire, cumin, salt, and pepper and stir to combine.

Transfer 1 ½ cups of the mixture to a blender and puree on high speed until broken down but not completely smooth, 15 to 20 seconds. Return the pureed mixture to the bowl and stir to combine.

Cover the soup and refrigerate for at least 2 hours and up to 12 hours. To serve, ladle the soup into bowls and garnish with basil leaves and cherry tomatoes.

KEEPING SUPPERS SIMPLE

SMALL TALK: *Keep gatherings small enough so that you can actually talk to all of your guests.*

SOURCE YOUR BAKED GOODS: *Breads and desserts can take a lot of time. When buying baked goods, it is important that they are made the morning of the purchase. Flaky pastry prepared with honey can get soggy if allowed to sit too long.*

TRIED-AND-TRUE RECIPES: *Make dishes you have whipped up at least once or twice before.*

QUALITY OVER QUANTITY: *Focus on quality ingredients and straightforward fare. Simple food speaks for itself.*

CATHY'S PARTY-READY PANTRY

Butter
Caviar
Cipriani dried pasta
Club soda
Eggs
Olives
Parmigiano Reggiano cheese
Pepperidge Farm Very Thin bread
Pimento cheese
Rao's homemade marinara sauce
Rosé
Veuve Clicquot

A SEASIDE SUPPER

Bethany McCann

Bethany McCann relishes playing hostess to friends. Whether organizing tea for two or throwing a New Year's Day buffet for fifty, the gregarious hostess is always on board. When late spring weather brings the irresistible urge to dine outdoors, she and her husband, Mike, host an alfresco dinner. Their expansive Galveston Bay compound, complete with commanding views of the water and bordering yacht club, is an ideal location for entertaining.

On this occasion, they gather guests to celebrate the start of sailing season. The sport is an integral part of their life and social circle. Mike, as well as all five of their kids, sailed competitively in high school, college, and beyond. "Thank goodness my job is planning the party," Bethany laughs. "I am the only one in the family who is not a sailor. I make a better first mate."

Rather than opting for the typical nautical theme with shades of red and blue, the hostess takes inspiration from summer flowers and her china cabinet. She elects to use a color palette that is fresh and unexpected. Soft, summery hues and thoughtful details abound. Always looking to keep the table-top interesting by adding sentimental touches, Bethany selects large coral-colored Mottahedeh plates to pair with her paternal grandmother's blue wreath Empire Rosenthal china. A mix of Reed & Barton Tara sterling flatware from her mother and International Royal Danish from her maternal grandmother flank the antique dinnerware.

Flickering votive candles, custom Jacquelyn Reese napkins, colored glassware, and unique accessories add a graceful touch to the outdoor dining table. Silver sailing trophies brimming with watermelon-colored ranunculus, coral dahlias, deep pink peonies, orange tulips, and white hydrangeas line the sixteen-foot table draped in a Schumacher outdoor fabric. Much to the surprise and delight of the invitees, several of the sterling trophies belong to her guests. "I had to be sly in procuring the cups," Bethany confesses. "I felt it was a fun way to acknowledge their accomplishments and elevate the table."

After rum gum cocktails and conversation by the pool, guests gather at the table. Dinner is the brainchild of a local chef from a neighboring yacht club. Together he and Bethany devised a seasonal menu to focus on local fish and produce. Grilled Texas peaches, goat cheese, and candied pecans rest atop fresh peppery arugula. Sweetly flavored Gulf Coast redfish pairs perfectly with ginger carrot puree for the main course. In keeping with Bethany's sentimental touches, the meal ends with a delectable pecan pie, a dessert that both her mother and grandmother adored.

RUM GUM

Serves 8

Rum is one of the world's oldest distilled spirits. It has a colorful history mired in colonialism and organized crime. Today, however, it is a summertime darling, and many yacht clubs have developed their own signature rum drinks. More often than not, each unique concoction is a tightly guarded secret. Luckily, Bethany was able to create her own adaption of the Texas Corinthian Yacht Club's rum gum. For the best results, look for artisanal and higher-proof rums.

4 ¼ cups strained freshly squeezed orange juice
1 ½ cups pineapple juice
2 cups gold rum, preferably Mount Gay
½ cup freshly squeezed lime juice
1 tablespoon simple syrup
8 lime slices

In a large pitcher, stir together the orange juice, pineapple juice, rum, lime juice, and simple syrup.

Refrigerate until chilled.

Serve over ice in lowball glasses. Garnish each glass with a lime slice.

RECOGNIZING RUM

WHITE: *White rum has no color and a mild flavor. It has a lighter body than gold and dark rums. This type of light rum is most often used to create cocktails that do not need a bold rum flavor.*

GOLD: *As rum mellows in the barrel, it takes on an amber or golden hue. Gold rum has more flavor than white rum and is used to make cocktails with a stronger flavor. Gold rums are often enjoyed neat or on the rocks.*

DARK: *Dark rums are aged in charred oak barrels and flavors are added. This gives the rum a dark color, heavy texture, and a complex flavor. Black rum is also known as dark rum and is aged the longest. Dark rum is used in many tiki drinks.*

SPICED: *Spicing rum was once little more than a cheap way of masking poor-quality spirits with overpowering flavors. Today there are many fine versions of spiced rum on the market. Roots of ginger, seeds of vanilla, allspice, bark of cinnamon or cassia, and buds of clove are commonly used as flavoring agents for spiced rums.*

GRILLED PEACHES, GOAT CHEESE, AND CANDIED PECAN SALAD

Serves 4

It is hard to improve upon the flavor of a ripe summer peach, unless you place it on a hot grill. Grilling caramelizes the fruit, making it even sweeter. For the best result, avoid grilling peaches that are too ripe. The fruit needs to be ripe, but firm, so that it can stand up to the heat of the grill without falling apart.

4 ripe but firm peaches, halved and pitted
½ tablespoon grapeseed oil
5 ounces baby arugula
½ cup Candied Pecans (recipe follows)
½ cup large chunks goat cheese
½ cup Honey Dijon Vinaigrette (recipe follows)

Prepare a gas or charcoal grill to medium heat (you should be able to hold your hand 1 inch above the cooking grate for 3 to 4 seconds before pulling it away from the heat).

Lightly brush the peaches with the grapeseed oil. Place the oiled peaches skin side down on the medium hot grill.

Cook the peaches until grill marks form, 2 to 3 minutes per side. Remove them from the grill and set aside.

Place the arugula in a large bowl with the pecans, goat cheese, and grilled peaches.

Lightly toss with the dressing and serve immediately on individual plates.

Note: Lightly oil the grill to prevent the peaches from sticking.

CANDIED PECANS
Makes ½ cup

1 tablespoon unsalted butter
½ cup pecan halves
1 tablespoon brown sugar
1 pinch sea salt

Melt the butter in a small frying pan over low heat. Add the pecans, brown sugar, and sea salt.

Cook for 2 to 3 minutes, stirring constantly, until the sugar has caramelized and the pecans are coated.

Spread the pecans on wax paper to cool.

HONEY DIJON VINAIGRETTE
Makes ½ cup

1 tablespoon honey
2 teaspoons Dijon mustard
2 tablespoons Champagne vinegar
¼ cup extra-virgin olive oil
Salt and freshly ground black pepper to taste

Whisk the honey, mustard, and vinegar together in a medium-size bowl.

Slowly whisk in the olive oil in a steady stream until it is emulsified. Season with salt and pepper. Set aside.

HOLIDAYS AND
BIG DEAL MEALS

A PLAYFUL PURPLE PARTY
Courtnay Tartt Elias

Courtnay Tartt Elias is no shrinking violet. Her legendary soirees are as richly vibrant as her personality and Houston residence. She is known for her love of color, and especially her fearless use of purple—a color often associated with creativity, splendor, and devotion. All are traits that seem appropriate when describing this vivacious interior designer.

The home she shares with her husband, Mark, is the epicenter for engaging family and friends. For the dynamic duo, entertaining is never a small affair. Colleagues, kids, acquaintances, neighbors—everyone loves dropping in for a visit. Both Courtnay and Mark know exactly how to provide a fabulous feast with effortless elegance. Their strategy? Divide and conquer. Mark takes over the grill and Courtnay tackles the sides.

When it comes to the menu, they like to keep their guests guessing. On this occasion, they invited everyone over for a "low-key" dinner. Much to the delight and surprise of all in attendance, the couple then pulls out all of the stops and fêtes friends with a formal table and an old school menu. Blood orange romaine salad, roasted purple new potatoes, grilled corn, brisket, sausage, crème brûlée, and assorted artisanal macarons in rich plum hues grace the table.

Chic, colorful, and collected are the underlying principles of Courtnay's tabletop selections. A hand-embroidered periwinkle Mexican Otomi tablecloth is the jumping off point for the party. It is one of many in her collection. Over the summer she purchased several at the Santa Fe International Folk Art Market for such an occasion.

"People underestimate the power of purple," she sighs. "A table should be playful and a dinner party should be fun." Lavender, violet, amethyst, and mauve are just a few of the shades in the evening lineup. Richard Ginori Rapallo china is the star of the show. Swans, flowers, and ribbons, in shades of purple and pink against metallic gold accents, adorn the dinnerware. The service was a christening gift from Courtnay's godmother. By the time she was twelve years old, Courtnay owned a complete dessert set, including cake stands and powdered sugar shakers.

In lieu of a large flower arrangement, the hostess turned to her friend Jeff for a one-of-a-kind centerpiece. A clear glass vessel filled with a vibrant assortment of farmer's market produce takes center stage alongside complementary blooms and rare orchids from his garden. White-veined, red-leaf radicchio was the color inspiration. Massive grapes, artichokes, radishes, and basil act as supporting players. The monochromatic palette lends a cohesive feel. As a parting gift, everyone leaves with a few of the orchids—a meaningful and personal touch to end the evening.

THE POWER
OF PURPLE

Purple can be both dramatic and understated, depending on the hue or shade. It is a fun, versatile, and calming color.

Think of purple as a neutral. You can pair it with almost any color—black, red, yellow, orange, and chartreuse are particularly apt partners. The regal pigment can add richness to any space or drama to a simple room.

A palette ranging from light lavenders to deep plums and a few strategically placed accents are all you need to create a festive atmosphere. Purple works well with natural elements like seagrass or bamboo, and it looks equally good with metallics or marble.

Warm purples can make a dining room feel cozy, while dark, rich shades provide an exquisite backdrop for crystal and silver. Use purple accessories to brighten up a table and add depth to a neutral color scheme.

ROASTED PURPLE POTATOES WITH TARRAGON

Serves 6

In South America, purple potatoes are considered a food of the gods. Their unique, vibrant color and health benefits are making them increasingly popular in the United States, and these days most supermarkets and farmer's markets offer eye-catching assortments of the purple spuds. Adirondack blue, purple creamer, and purple majesty are just a few of the varieties. In addition to their fun shades, they are an excellent source of potassium, vitamin C, vitamin B6, and the antioxidant anthocyanin.

1 ½ pounds purple potatoes, quartered
3 tablespoons white truffle oil
3 large sprigs fresh tarragon, leaves removed and finely chopped
1 ½ teaspoons kosher salt
1 teaspoon cracked black pepper
Fresh rosemary sprigs for garnish, optional

Preheat the oven to 350°F.

In a large bowl, toss the potatoes with the truffle oil, tarragon, salt, and pepper.

Transfer the potato mixture to a sheet pan and roast in the preheated oven for 25 minutes. Flip the potatoes and roast until fork-tender and lightly charred, about 15 additional minutes. Transfer to a large dish and serve immediately.

GRILLED CORN ON THE COB

Serves 8

8 medium ears sweet corn, in the husk
1 stick (8 tablespoons) unsalted butter, softened
3 tablespoons minced fresh basil
1 tablespoon minced fresh flat-leaf parsley
½ teaspoon sea salt
1 cup grated cotija cheese or crumbled feta cheese

Place the corn in a stockpot. Add cold water to cover. Soak for 20 minutes, then drain. Prepare a gas or charcoal grill to medium heat.

Carefully peel back the corn husks to within 1 inch from the bottom of the husk. Remove the silk.

In a small bowl, mix the butter, basil, parsley, and salt until thoroughly combined. Spread the butter mixture over the corn.

Rewrap the corn in the husks. Tie the husks closed with kitchen twine.

Grill the corn over medium heat, turning frequently, until tender, 25 to 30 minutes.

Cut the twine and peel back the husks. Sprinkle with cotija or feta cheese.

SELECTING AND GRILLING CORN ON THE COB

The best way to select corn on the cob is to pull back the husks. Look to see if the kernels are evenly spaced and consistent in size and color. Look for tassels that are yellowish brown and sticky to the touch.

Discard corn with small brown wormholes in the husk. If you cannot peel back the husk, use your fingers to feel the kernels through the husk. Make certain the kernels feel plump and plentiful.

A corn husk should be bright green and tightly wrapped. A yellow or dry husk is a sign of older corn.

DINNER AT THE STORK CLUB
Carla McDonald

The Golden Age of Hollywood—the phrase alone conjures up fun, frivolity, and glamour. Perhaps only Manhattan's legendary Stork Club can invoke a similar sense of bewitchment, gaiety, and fascination. The chic, sleek private club was the brainchild of ex-bootlegger and Oklahoma native Sherman Billingsley. From its opening in 1929 to its demise in 1965, it was the place for celebrities and aristocrats to see and be seen. The news of Grace Kelly's engagement to Prince Rainier of Monaco first broke at the famous oasis.

"I would have loved to dine at the Stork Club," confides Carla McDonald. "It was an historic establishment in a different day and age." Bing Crosby, the Duke and Duchess of Windsor, Ernest Hemingway, Gloria Vanderbilt, J. Edgar Hoover, J. D. Salinger, and Babe Paley were all patrons. But rather than dwell on the past, Carla, founder of *The Salonniere*, a website dedicated to the art of entertaining, draws upon it to reinterpret an evening at the famed institution. This is, after all, the woman whose mantra is "I feel a party coming on." Friends cannot help but be excited and intrigued when they receive heavy cardstock invitations modeled on the club's original, iconic stork logo in shades of emerald green. It is clear that Carla lives by the old adage: The devil is in the details.

As Carla's guests arrive, she greets each one with a hug and a signature cocktail. Tonight everyone is greeted with the Stork Club's classic concoction—gin, Cointreau, Angostura bitters, and freshly squeezed orange and lime juices. "I like to offer my guests a drink the minute they walk in," says Carla. "Everyone feels more comfortable at a party with a drink in hand." Gin is the hostess's "giggle water" of choice.

Rows and rows of flickering glass candleholders, reminiscent of the table lamps used at the celebrated club, run the length of the dining table. Fresh gardenias, a flower popular in the Stork Club era, adorn each place setting in the dining room. Green Baccarat water glasses and gold-rimmed Champagne coupes reflect the soft chandelier lighting, adding to the glamour of the evening. Black-and-white photographs of Old Hollywood celebrities, whom dinner guests resemble, are slipped into vintage silver frames and used as visual place cards, requiring guests to seek out their lookalikes. "It makes finding your seat so much more fun, and it is a great icebreaker," Carla explains.

Friends are treated to pan-seared halibut over wilted spinach and duck à la Dietrich, a cheeky interpretation of a famous club dish. After dinner, guests move into the living room for Champagne and truffles, or to the Bordeaux-lacquered library for Scotch and cookie "cigars" presented in vintage Stork Club ashtrays. After the last guest departs, Carla slips off her heels and curls up on the sofa with her husband to recap the evening and revel in the memories they created. "Parties are fun, but they are also important," Carla asserts. "No one can survive without meaningful human connections."

DINNER

at the

Stork Club

FIRST

Pan-Seared Halibut
sauce choron & wilted spinach

ENTRÉE

Duck à la Dietrich
poached peach & red wine syrup

RUSSIAN BLINIS
WITH CAVIAR

Makes 2 dozen

A staple in traditional Russian cooking, the blini
is as versatile as it is enduring. Made from
buckwheat flour and served with caviar, it is both
delicious and decadent.

⅔ cup all-purpose flour
½ cup buckwheat flour
½ teaspoon salt
1 teaspoon instant or rapid-rise yeast
1 cup warm milk
2 tablespoons unsalted butter, melted and cooled
1 large egg, room temperature, separated
1 pint crème fraîche
4 to 6 ounces caviar
Chopped dill, and lemon rind and wedges,
　 as accompaniments

In a large bowl mix together the all-purpose flour,
buckwheat flour, salt, and instant yeast. Make a
well in the center. Pour in milk and mix until
smooth. Cover with a dishtowel and let rise until
the batter doubles in size, about 1 hour.

Stir the butter and the egg yolk into the batter. In a
separate bowl, whisk the egg white until stiff, but
not dry. Fold the egg white into the batter. Cover
the bowl with a cloth and let stand 20 minutes.

Heat a nonstick skillet over medium heat.
Drop quarter-size dollops of batter into the
skillet without overcrowding (you will need
to work in batches). Cook the pancakes until
bubbles form on the surface and break,
about 1 minute. Turn the pancakes and cook
for 30 seconds on the opposite side.

Remove the pancakes from the skillet to a large
dish and cover with a dishtowel to keep warm.
Repeat with the remaining batter. To serve,
top each blini with a spoonful of crème fraîche
and a little caviar. Serve with chopped dill and
lemon rind and wedges on the side.

CARLA'S STORK CLUB COCKTAIL

Serves 1

The Stork Club's chief barman, Nathaniel "Cookie" Cook, invented dozens of drinks for the club. He also created its signature libation. The Stork Club cocktail featured sweetened Old Tom gin, freshly squeezed orange and lime juices, Cointreau, and bitters. The drink was tangy, popular, and quaffable. Plus, the tangerine-hued cocktail added a splash of color to the club's dark-paneled dining room.

1 ½ ounces (3 tablespoons) Ransom Old Tom gin
1 ounce (2 tablespoons) freshly squeezed
    orange juice
¼ ounce (1 ½ teaspoons) freshly squeezed
    lime juice
¼ ounce (1 ½ teaspoons) Cointreau
1 dash Angostura bitters
1 orange twist

Pour the liquid ingredients into an ice-filled cocktail shaker. Shake well. Strain the mixture into a chilled Champagne coupe. Garnish with the orange twist.

PLAYING FAVORITES

BAR ACCESSORIES: *Vintage, Asprey*
CANDLE: *Diptyque Figuier*
CAVIAR: *osetra*
CHAMPAGNE: *Krug Rosé*
CHINA: *Alberto Pinto, Bernardaud, Philippe Deshoulieres, Mottahedeh*
COOKBOOKS: Mastering the Art of French Cooking *by Julia Child,* The New York Times Cookbook *by Craig Claiborne*
CRYSTAL: *Saint-Louis, Theresienthal, Lalique, Baccarat*
EVERYDAY DINNERWARE: *Juliska Bamboo, Bernardaud Naxos*
EVERYDAY GLASSWARE: *Juliska*
FLATWARE: *Christofle*
FLOWERS: *peonies*
GIN: *Monkey 47, Hendrick's*
GUEST SOAP: *Jo Malone grapefruit body and hand wash*
LINENS: *Julia B., Léron, E. Braun & Co.*
ONLINE FOOD SOURCES: *Frog Hollow Farm, D'Artagnan, iGourmet*
PARTY-READY PANTRY ESSENTIALS: *marcona almonds, rice crackers, popcorn, and truffle salt*
STATIONERY: *Mrs. John L. Strong, Connor, The Printery (Oyster Bay, New York)*
TABLETOP ACCESSORIES: *Buccellati, Tiffany & Co.*
VODKA: *Tito's, Belvedere, Crystal Head*
WINE: *white Burgundy*

DELICACIES OF THE DEEP

Michael Harold and Quinn Peeper

Famous for Creole cuisine, a distinctive dialect, French architecture, famed festivals, and legendary jazz music, New Orleans is a city like no other. Whether it is magnificent homes or merrymakers in the streets, all of the city's aspects combine to make it endlessly interesting.

"Interesting" is also an adjective that aptly describes Michael Harold and Quinn Peeper. Michael, an attorney, and Quinn, a doctor, both are accomplished hosts, concert pianists, and seasoned antiques collectors. This power pair knows precisely how to throw a party and assemble fascinating company. Moreover, both have a unique talent for making visitors feel treasured and transported in time. From artists to statesmen, all are invited to their frequent soirees.

Michael and Quinn's 1863 shotgun double camelback-style New Orleans home is their favorite place to entertain. Two structures converted into one, it is as grand and unique as its inhabitants. Filled with unusual objects, ornate oil paintings, antiques from the estate of Keith Irvine, and Vieux Paris porcelain, the atmosphere feels very much like that of an eighteenth-century salon. Evenings are designed partially to amuse and partially to enhance the knowledge of participants through conversation.

Michael, a New Orleans native and fantastic cook, loves to showcase the cuisine of his beloved city. With marshy waters just outside the city, teeming with fish, crab, crawfish, and oysters, New Orleans is a seafood town. "When family and friends visit, the last thing they want is something they can get at home," Michael acknowledges. With a fresh seafood market within walking distance, guests are never disappointed.

At most of Michael and Quinn's dinner parties, Creole cuisine and Cajun influences prevail. On the menu for their delicacies of the deep party (a theme borrowed from a New Orleans carnival krewe), gumbo makes an appearance. Like most Louisiana dishes, gumbo starts with what locals call "the holy trinity." This unpretentious mix of chopped celery, green pepper, and onion packs a punch of flavor.

While the gumbo simmers, Quinn bedecks the dining room table with Bernardaud Elysée china, William Yeoward Cora crystal etched with a custom crest, and pieces from his grandmother. "It pays to be the favorite grandchild," Quinn laughs. "Also, never discount the power of eBay when it comes to finding treasures no one else wants."

The evening is a beautiful example of collaboration. Or, as biologist Richard Dawkins noted, "Creatures with complementary skills flourish in each other's presence."

MICHAEL'S GUMBO

Serves 6 to 8

Michael's gumbo is a combination of several recipes. After years of experimenting and turning to local Junior League cookbooks, including *River Road Recipes, Jambalaya*, and *Talk About Good!*, he crafted his own foolproof version. Serve over white rice.

¾ cup vegetable oil
1 cup all-purpose flour
1 cup finely chopped onion
¾ cup finely chopped green bell pepper
¾ cup finely chopped celery
2 tablespoons minced garlic
7 cups seafood stock
One 5 ½-ounce can spicy vegetable juice,
    preferably V8
¼ teaspoon dried thyme
¼ teaspoon dried oregano
¼ teaspoon paprika
2 bay leaves
2 teaspoons Worcestershire sauce
1 ½ teaspoons salt
1 teaspoon freshly ground black pepper
½ teaspoon cayenne pepper

1 ½ pounds medium shrimp, peeled and deveined
1 pound cooked lump crabmeat
2 cups shucked oysters with their liquor
¼ cup chopped flat-leaf parsley
½ cup chopped tender green onion tops

Place an 8-quart stockpot over medium heat and add the oil. Allow the oil to heat for 5 minutes, then add the flour to the pot. Lower the heat to medium-low and stir the oil and flour constantly with a wooden spoon until it forms a roux the color of milk chocolate, 20 to 25 minutes.

Add the onion, bell pepper, and celery to the roux and stir to blend. Stir the vegetables for 5 minutes, then add the garlic. Cook the garlic for 30 seconds. Add the seafood stock, and spicy vegetable juice to the pot. Stir in the thyme, oregano, paprika, bay leaves, Worcestershire, salt, black pepper, and cayenne. Bring the mixture to a boil, then lower the heat to a simmer. Simmer for 1 hour, skimming off foam and any oil that rises to the surface.

Stir in the shrimp and cook for 2 minutes. Add the lump crabmeat and the oysters with their liquor. Cook for 5 minutes, stirring frequently, then remove from the heat (keep an eye on the clock so that you do not overcook the oysters). Taste and adjust seasoning if necessary. Remove and discard bay leaves. Garnish with the parsley and green onions and serve in shallow bowls over white rice.

GREAT GUMBO

Of all the dishes in the realm of Louisiana cooking, gumbo is probably the most famous and likely the most popular. Although ingredients vary from one cook's recipe to the next, the fragrant bowl of goodness is as emblematic of Louisiana as lobster is of Maine.

THE HOLY TRINITY: *The holy trinity of Cajun and Creole cooking is made up of onion, celery, and bell pepper. This combination is the base for most savory dishes and more often than not is added to roux at the beginning of a stew, soup, or jambalaya. It is a Louisiana variant of a French mirepoix (usually made with onion, celery, and carrot). A typical trinity includes 2 cups chopped onion, 1 ½ cups chopped celery, and 1 ¼ cups chopped green bell pepper.*

ROUX: *The key to a great gumbo is the roux. Two simple ingredients—oil and flour—are transformed over heat. Stirring is crucial to avoid burning the roux. Stir constantly over medium-low heat until the mixture becomes dark brown and takes on a nutty smell. A light roux should be the color of caramel, while a dark roux will take on the color of chocolate or mud. The darker the roux, the richer the flavor.*

TYPES: *Gumbo is usually made with whatever protein is on hand or in season. There are boundless variations and all yield delectable results. Shrimp and okra gumbo is a perennial favorite, as is chicken and okra gumbo. Other successful pairings include seafood and sausage; shrimp and crab; turkey and andouille; and pork and tasso. Turkey and sausage gumbos appear frequently during Thanksgiving and Christmas.*

WHAT IS THE DIFFERENCE BETWEEN GUMBO AND JAMBALAYA? *Jambalaya is primarily a rice dish, similar to paella, while gumbo is a stew that is thickened with roux, okra, or filé powder.*

CRAB MAISON

Serves 4

Galatoire's restaurant in New Orleans is a beloved institution, and Crab Maison is one of its most popular appetizers. Reportedly, the restaurant uses up to 750 pounds of lump crabmeat each week, much of which ends up in this popular dish. Michael has adapted this favorite recipe for the home cook. Serve with crackers and sliced French bread.

½ cup mayonnaise, preferably real mayonnaise
2 tablespoons light olive oil
2 teaspoons white wine vinegar
1 teaspoon Creole mustard (you may substitute
   Dijon or seeded mustard)
1 teaspoon small capers, rinsed and drained
½ teaspoon finely chopped flat-leaf parsley
½ teaspoon kosher salt
⅛ teaspoon freshly ground white pepper
3 green onions, finely chopped
1 pound jumbo lump crabmeat
Large butter lettuce leaves for garnish

Whisk together the mayonnaise, oil, vinegar, mustard, capers, parsley, salt, pepper, and green onions. Gently fold in the crabmeat.

Line a serving bowl or platter with the lettuce leaves. Spoon the crab mixture over the leaves and serve.

ASTUTO
BOLGHERI SUPERIORE

BARONE
RICASOLI

DELICACIES OF THE DEEP
NEW ORLEANS, LOUISIANA

MENU

CRABMEAT POT DE CREME

ROASTED OYSTERS CREOLE

LOUISIANA CRAWFISH AND CRAB GUMBO

BANANAS FOSTER WITH VANILLA ICE CREAM

TURKISH DELIGHT

FRIENDS AND FIREWORKS
Danielle Rollins

White butterfly bushes, flickering gas lanterns, and baskets filled with red honeysuckle attract more than butterflies, bees, and hummingbirds to the gracious garden of Danielle Rollins. It is also the lively destination for a plein air Fourth of July dinner with friends. The lifestyle maven is renowned for her fabled parties, culinary competence, and fearless approach to design. She revels in playful patterns and color—especially white and blue. This classic combination is spot on for such a celebration.

Whether at work or at play, Danielle is an adventurous soul. When it comes to gardening and entertaining she is a buoyant spirit. The lavish Atlanta home she shares with her family, three dogs, and one cat is a design laboratory. It is a place for her to learn, make mistakes, and have fun. A maze of sphere-shaped boxwoods had a few people scratching their heads when she first proposed the idea. Now mature, it is the star of the yard. "The non-traditional planting makes me happy every time I walk out the door," she smiles. Today an American flag waves above the fanciful shrubs to mark the occasion.

An allée of flowering Natchez crepe myrtles lines the driveway and greets arriving guests. One by one friends enter the garden, then quickly swap shorts and sundresses for swimsuits. It is a day for Danielle to regale friends. A cheerful libation is served poolside. Sauvignon Blanc and a berry-flavored vodka are the basis of the summery sangria. Paper straws, fresh mid-summer mint, and local berries add a spirited touch.

As the afternoon slides into evening, everyone dresses for dinner and gathers around the festive outdoor dinner table. Danielle's own fabric, a stylized ikat in soft red and ivory, serves as a cheerful and elegant backdrop for a fanciful tabletop. In keeping with the colors of the season, the hostess uses blue glass votive cups, red Lenox tumblers, and clear La Rochère glasses. Bright white Walker Valentine linens, trimmed in red, sit atop blue-and-white-striped plates. Humble hydrangeas take center stage, adding texture and a punch of color.

The Independence Day menu includes some of Danielle's very favorite summertime specialties— deviled eggs, fried chicken, cornbread, and a radish-laced salad. Homemade pies round out the meal. The cherry and blueberry pies are all-star crowd pleasers.

After dinner the adults linger over glasses of wine, then head to the lawn for a twilight tête-à-tête. Children light sparklers and trace their names against the night sky. A colorful explosion of fireworks erupts in the distance, followed by applause—it is the final exclamation point to a banner celebration.

DINING OUTDOORS

In the spirit of the season, Danielle shares her favorite ideas for festive outdoor entertaining.

Look for ample shade so that your guests are comfortable.

Select a visually pleasing location with trees, flowers, and greenery.

Choose an intimate space to create a cocoon-like feel around the table.

A self-serve bar is perfect for an outdoor lunch or dinner. Keep linen cocktail napkins stacked in basket trays.

Use an outdoor urn as an ice bucket and an ice bucket to hold flowers from the garden.

Think of your space as an indoor dining room. Select chairs that are comfortable, stylish, and durable.

Personalized paperweights make great outdoor place cards. They will not blow away and guests can take them home as parting gifts.

DANIELLE'S SUMMER SANGRIA

Makes 8 cups

Little is known about the origins of the Spanish drink sangria. It was introduced to the United States in the late 1940s and enjoyed great popularity at the 1964 World's Fair in New York. Sangria traditionally consists of wine and chopped fruit. It can also include orange juice, orange-flavored liqueur, or brandy. For this recipe, Danielle uses white wine rather than the typical red.

2 bottles Sauvignon Blanc
1 cup triple sec
½ cup berry-flavored vodka, such as
    Cîroc red berry vodka
½ cup freshly squeezed lemon juice
½ cup simple syrup
2 cups blueberries
2 cups strawberries, hulled and sliced
1 cup raspberries

Combine all of the ingredients in a large pitcher and stir well. Cover the pitcher with plastic wrap and refrigerate for at least 4 hours. Serve over ice in tumblers.

CHERRY PIE

Serves 6

Pies are a slice of Americana. Come summer, everybody saves room for the flaky pastry. Since mid-summer cherry harvesting coincides with Independence Day, cherry pie is the perfect dessert to serve on this occasion.

FILLING
2 tablespoons cornstarch
2 tablespoons water
2 cups sweet cherries, such as Bing, pitted
Three 14.5-ounce cans sour cherries in water (not syrup)
1 cup sugar
1 tablespoon pure vanilla extract
1 tablespoon almond extract
1 tablespoon ground cinnamon

CRUST
2 cups all-purpose flour, sifted, plus more for dusting
1 teaspoon kosher salt
¼ teaspoon sugar
2 sticks unsalted butter, cold and cut into pieces
¼ cup ice water
1 large egg
1 tablespoon milk

To make the filling, in a small bowl, combine the cornstarch and water. Stir until the cornstarch dissolves.

Place the fresh cherries in a large bowl. Drain the juice from the canned cherries into a medium saucepan. Add the drained cherries to the bowl of fresh cherries.

Add the sugar to the saucepan with the cherry juice. Bring to a simmer and cook over medium heat until reduced to 1 ½ cups, about 30 minutes. Stir frequently to prevent the bottom from burning. Reduce the heat to medium-low. Stirring constantly, add the cornstarch mixture. Bring to a boil. Cook, stirring constantly, until the cherry juice mixture becomes translucent.

Remove the cherry filling from the heat. Spoon a little of the filling onto a plate. Allow to cool slightly. Rub it between your fingertips to feel for any remaining grains of cornstarch. If necessary, cook slightly longer to dissolve the cornstarch.

Transfer the filling to a large bowl and fold in the cherries. Then, stir in the vanilla extract and cinnamon. Allow to cool completely.

For the crust, in a large bowl, combine the flour, salt, and sugar. Cut in the butter with a fork or pastry knife until the mixture resembles coarse crumbs. Stir in the water, 1 tablespoon at a time, until mixture forms a ball. Divide the dough into two equal balls, wrap in plastic wrap, and chill the dough in the refrigerator for 1 hour.

Preheat the oven to 400°F.

Remove the dough from the refrigerator. On a floured surface, roll out the dough balls into two flat ⅛-inch-thick pieces for the top and bottom crusts of the pie. They should be about 10 inches in diameter.

Carefully transfer the bottom crust to a 9-inch pie pan and arrange it so it lines the bottom and sides. Let the edges hang over the edge of the pan. Pour the cherry mixture into the dough-lined pie pan. Cover the filled pie with the second piece of dough. Pinch the dough edges together to seal and crimp decoratively. Cut away any excess dough. Using a sharp knife, cut five to six 2-inch slits in the top of the crust. Start the slits in the center and continue toward the edges.

Mix the egg and milk in a small bowl with a fork until combined. Brush the surface of the dough with the egg wash.

Bake the pie on the bottom rack of the preheated oven for 20 minutes. Lower the heat to 375°F. Move the pie to the center rack, and bake until the crust is golden and the filling begins to bubble, 20 to 25 additional minutes.

Transfer the pie to a rack to cool. Serve 2 to 3 hours after baking.

THANKSGIVING
IN NEW ENGLAND
Lisa Hilderbrand

The rambling 240-year-old New England farmhouse Lisa Hilderbrand shares with her husband Eric, and their sons, Patrick and Robert, sits quietly next to the Silvermine River in New Canaan, Connecticut, a picturesque town settled in the early eighteenth century. Though the home was in great disarray during their original viewing, Lisa was not deterred. The antiques dealer and interior designer instantly fell in love with the decrepit structure. Seeing possibilities over problems, she forged ahead and created a functioning family home. Lisa was especially charmed by its history, and the original planked floors and seven hearths.

The 7,200-square-foot clapboard house is fashioned from several additions, the last added in 1927. Boasting a vast dining room with wide, hand-planed pine paneling, chamfered ceiling beams, and a fireplace, it was made for formal feasts. Although the space is dark and moody during the day, it is magical at night. A roaring fire and glowing candlelight add warmth and coziness.

Thanksgiving, perhaps the most American of all holidays, is the perfect day for Lisa to indulge her love of hosting big dinners and laboring over every minute detail. From selecting the menu and setting the table to arranging the flowers and choosing the music, she relishes it all. Cocktails and dinner tunes start with the strains of jazz saxophonist Stan Getz pulsating in the distance, followed by Paul Desmond, Sergio Mendes and Brasil '66, and then bossa nova genius João Gilberto.

For added ambiance, the hostess uses an abundance of candles to light the room. Tall candlesticks resting in candelabras, pillar candles placed inside hurricane lamps, and small votives, scattered across the table, all twinkle in the dark. Antique Fitzhugh china, sitting atop mirrored placemats, moves the light around the room. The effect is festive and dramatic. Before dinner the kids warm up with mugs of hot apple cider, while the adults enjoy cocktails by a crackling fire.

The feast showcases a bounty of beloved recipes. Traditional dishes include sweet potatoes, mashed potatoes, cranberry relish, green beans, Brussels sprouts with bacon, stuffing, pies, and, of course, a perfectly roasted turkey. "This is not the meal to substitute low-fat options," Lisa laughs. Plenty of bottles of Goldeneye Pinot Noir, a family favorite, are on hand. For the Hilderbrands, it is a day when everyone can linger over dinner, enjoy another glass of wine, and be as boisterous and as gluttonous as they desire. After the meal, everyone retires to the living room to watch a game of football. It is the perfect way to end a celebration of family, friends, and cherished foods that evoke happy memories.

TIPS FOR PERFECT MASHED POTATOES

While mashed potatoes are very forgiving, these tips will help to produce perfect potatoes every time.

Use Yukon gold potatoes. These yellow-fleshed potatoes have a rich, almost buttery taste and are perfect for mashing.

Boil potatoes in large pieces. Small pieces allow more water to make its way inside the tubers, resulting in a less flavorful final product.

Keep potatoes hot. For a creamy taste and texture, do not let the potatoes cool before mashing. As soon as the potatoes have been boiled and drained, use heavy dish gloves to handle the hot spuds and mash them right away.

Fat goes first. Add butter or olive oil to potatoes before adding any liquid. This ensures that the texture remains firm before being softened by milk or cream.

Do not add all the liquid at once. Potatoes cannot absorb large amounts of liquid all at once. Adding smaller amounts of milk or cream, a little at a time, creates greater creaminess.

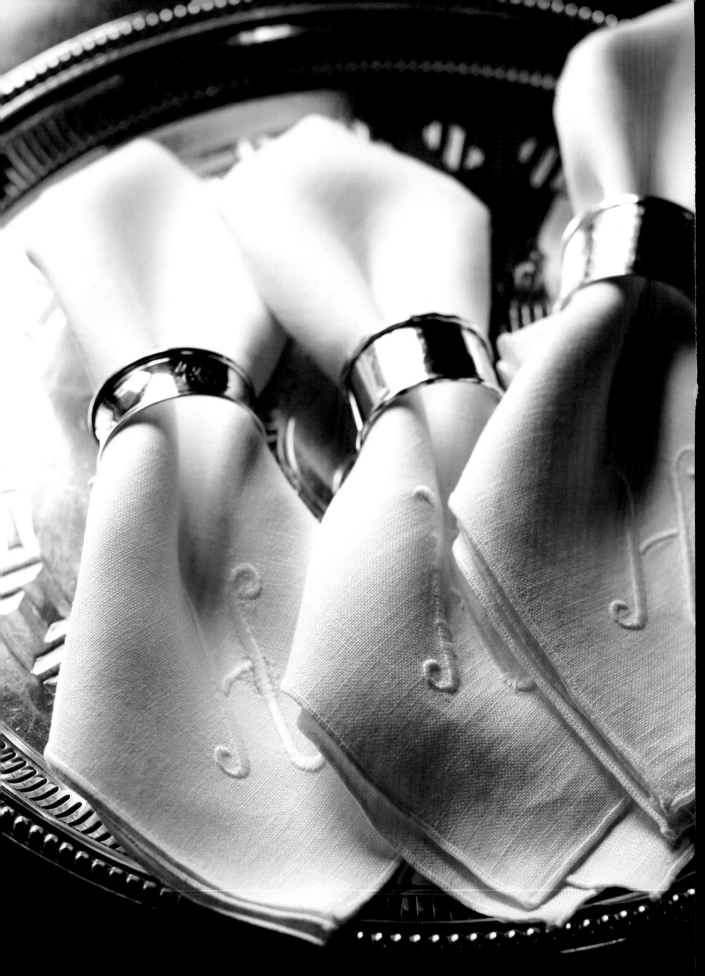

OLD-FASHIONED SWEET POTATOES

Serves 6

This dish is a family favorite and a nod to Lisa's Southern upbringing. Sweet potatoes topped with apples, golden raisins, and gooey marshmallows grace most Southern Thanksgiving tables. Sometimes this dish makes a Christmas appearance, too. Watch carefully when broiling the marshmallows. Just as with a campfire, under the broiler they go from perfectly brown to burnt to a crisp in the blink of an eye.

6 large, long sweet potatoes, unpeeled
1 teaspoon kosher salt
5 tablespoons salted butter
1 Granny Smith apple, peeled, cored, and thinly sliced
3 tablespoons light brown sugar
½ cup plus 1 tablespoon golden raisins
6 large marshmallows, halved

Wash the potatoes and cut into 1 ½-inch-thick rounds. Place the rounds in a pot and add enough cold water to cover. Add the salt to the water and bring to a gentle boil. Simmer until just tender when pierced with a fork. Do not allow the potatoes to fall apart.

Preheat the oven to 350°F.

While the potatoes are boiling, melt 2 tablespoons of the butter in a small pan. Sauté the apple slices until lightly golden. Set aside.

Drain the potatoes and allow them to cool slightly. Once cool enough to handle, peel off the skins.

Arrange about ⅓ of the potatoes in a single layer in a deep baking dish. Sprinkle with 1 tablespoon brown sugar and dot with 1 tablespoon butter cut into small pieces. Arrange one apple slice on each potato slice, using about ⅓ of the slices, then sprinkle with 3 tablespoons golden raisins. Repeat until you have three layers of potatoes, apples, and raisins.

Cover the dish with aluminum foil and bake in the preheated oven until the potatoes are tender and heated through, about 30 minutes. Remove from the oven. Preheat the broiler to low. Carefully remove the aluminum foil from the dish.

Place the marshmallow halves on top of the potatoes. Broil until the marshmallows turn golden brown, checking every 30 seconds or so and watching carefully, as marshmallows burn quickly. Serve immediately.

THANKSGIVING TURKEY TIPS

TRUSS LOOSELY: *Legs that are tied tightly against the sides of the turkey take longer to roast, putting the breast meat at risk of overcooking. Tying the turkey too tightly can also prevent the thighs from cooking evenly.*

THE PERFECT PAN: *Look for a heavy-duty stainless steel roasting pan with 2-inch sides. Sides that are too high prevent the lower part of the bird from browning properly and make basting difficult.*

THE RIGHT RUB: *Olive oil and melted clarified butter are two of the best rubs. Slather over the entire turkey to create even, brown skin. Then sprinkle with kosher salt (unless the turkey has been brined) to help crisp the skin.*

UPSIDE DOWN: *Place the turkey upside down in a roasting rack to collect the natural juices in the breast, which tends to be dry. After roasting for 1 hour, flip the turkey breast-side up to finish roasting. The marks on the breast from the rack will disappear as it continues to cook.*

AVOID BURNING THE BIRD: *If the bird is browning quickly, but is not near doneness (170°F), lightly tent the turkey loosely with foil and continue roasting.*

DELECTABLE DRIPPINGS: *Pan drippings make the best gravy. If the drippings are getting too dark, add a couple of tablespoons of water to keep them from burning.*

LET IT REST: *The intense heat of the oven forces the juices into the center of the bird. After roasting, let the turkey rest for roughly 20 minutes. The juices will redistribute, resulting in moist slices.*

MOTHER-DAUGHTER HOLIDAY TEA
Christy Ford

ew things are more magical than experiencing Christmastime through the eyes of a child. Just ask Christy Ford. Every year the sounds of little feet, seasonal songs from the *Home Alone* soundtrack, and lots of laughter reverberate through her Charlottesville home. On the day of her annual mother-daughter tea party, holiday merriment is at fever pitch.

The much-anticipated gathering began when Christy was a small girl. The yearly celebration became such a favorite of friends and family that it continued through her college days. At one point, attendance grew so large that people were invited in shifts to accommodate the growing guest list. "My mom took it to a level I have never been able to achieve," Christy sighs. "Father Christmas, dressed in ivory, would make a dramatic entrance, and a photographer would take pictures of each guest."

Now with her own daughters, Ruby and Tulip, the tradition not only lives on, but spans three generations. The youngest partygoers don their prettiest frocks for the festive occasion. "For my girls, a tea party is all about feeling fancy. It's velvet, lace, and tutus," she laughs.

Christy and her daughters bake gingerbread men and sugar cookie fairies, then decorate together. The same tableware she would use for an adult affair is employed. A large, rectangular dining table serves as a gathering place for cups, cookies, candy, cocoa, and candles. Trays of finger sandwiches, cranberry punch, Champagne, and, of course, tea await the arrival of friends.

Paperwhites, amaryllis, tulips, lilies, dusty miller, and seeded eucalyptus fill every corner. Hollow taper candles in chartreuse gently light the table. "Since we have so many colors going at Christmas I gravitate toward chartreuse, natural shades of green, and white flowers."

A tall Fraser fir in the alcove of a light-filled sunroom, twinkling with colorful lights, glass balls, and handmade ornaments, summons little ones. Long beams of winter sunlight shine through frosted windowpanes, adding an extra layer of sparkle. Oversized antique mirrors reflect Christmas wreaths, mistletoe, and a henhouse in the distance. The Ford's chickens provide eggs for all of their holiday baking, and more eggs are tucked into white porcelain egg holders as parting gifts. These thoughtful tokens provide happy memories of a beloved seasonal gathering.

In a large bowl, cream together the butter and sugar until smooth. Add the eggs, one at a time, beating to incorporate between additions, then beat in the vanilla. Beat in the flour, baking powder, and salt until combined. Cover with plastic wrap and refrigerate for at least 8 hours.

When you are ready to bake the cookies, preheat the oven to 400°F. Line cookie sheets with parchment paper. On a lightly floured surface, roll out the dough ¼- to ½ inch thick. Cut the dough into shapes with cookie cutters. Place the cookies 1 inch apart on the prepared pans.

Bake in the preheated oven until they are golden, 5 to 7 minutes. Watch the cookies closely to be sure they do not to burn. Cool completely on pans on a cooling rack.

SUGAR COOKIE ICING
Makes 2 cups

3 cups confectioners' sugar
2 to 4 tablespoons whole milk
2 teaspoons light corn syrup
1 teaspoon almond extract
Assorted food coloring

In a large bowl, combine the sugar and 2 tablespoons milk. Mix with an electric mixer until completely smooth. The icing should be a spreadable consistency, but not a thick paste. If you need to thin the icing, add 1 tablespoon of milk and combine. If it needs to be thinned further, add the remaining tablespoon.

Stir in the corn syrup and almond extract. Divide the icing into separate bowls for the number of colors desired for decorating.

Add food coloring to each bowl of icing, one drop at a time, until the desired color is reached. (Keep the icing tightly covered until ready to use. If you are leaving it in the bowl, be sure to cover the bowl with plastic wrap or the sugar will harden on the top.) Pour the icing into squeeze bottles or piping bags. Decorate the cookies and allow them to dry overnight.

ROLLED SUGAR COOKIES

Makes 4 to 5 dozen cookies, depending on size and shape

During the 1930s, it became a tradition for American children to leave sugar cookies and milk out for Santa Claus on Christmas Eve. The tasty treats made from easy-to-shape dough became wildly popular. Whether you go all-out with icing and decorations or opt for a few simple sprinkles, baking sugar cookies is a great way to usher in the holidays.

3 sticks unsalted butter, softened
3 cups sugar
4 large eggs
2 teaspoons vanilla extract
5 cups all-purpose flour
2 teaspoons baking powder
1 teaspoon salt

TEA SANDWICH TIPS
AND SUGGESTIONS

An array of delicate sandwiches makes an impressive presentation. Spread a very thin layer of soft butter on each slice of bread before adding toppings (this helps prevent sogginess). The bread used for tea sandwiches should be crustless, but do fill the sandwiches before removing the crusts. Slice the crusts off with a serrated knife, then cut sandwiches into batons or triangles.

SUGGESTED SANDWICHES

Smoked Salmon with Cream Cheese
Sliced Cucumber with Butter
Curried Egg Salad
Country Pâté
Chicken Salad
Avocado and Watercress
Apple Butter and Peanut Butter

CHRISTY ON
GIVING GIFTS

Keep gifts simple and thoughtful.

I love giving fresh eggs from our backyard chickens in white porcelain egg holders.

Place a bag of loose tea in a porcelain cup and pair with a box of homemade scones.

I adore collecting antique vessels and filling them with everyday objects. A few ideas include:

Fill a beautiful antique compote dish with baby Seckel pears.

Pile artisanal salts into antique salt cellars.

Decant small batches of good bourbon into vintage hand-cut crystal decanters.

CHRISTMAS DAY DINNER AND DESSERTS
Susan and Skylar Dabbar

As soon as the Dabbar Thanksgiving feast comes to an end, mother-and-daughter duo Susan and Skylar begin prepping and planning for the endless rounds of holiday dinners they host in their Washington, D.C., home. In the lead-up to the merriment and madness of the season, Susan stockpiles artisanal cheeses, crackers, preserves, and bottles of Sancerre. She also keeps her local butcher on speed dial. Skylar comes over on the weekends to create Christmas confections. The charismatic pair shares a passion for cooking and entertaining.

On the twenty-fifth of December their gastronomic prowess is on full display. The halls of their Wesley Heights house are filled with the aromas of the season: beef tenderloin, freshly baked popovers, roasted potatoes, fresh rosemary, and desserts. Skylar's cakes, crafted with spun sugar and frosted cranberries, are works of art. Crackling fires and an army of handcrafted Russian Santas, also known as Father Frost, bid greetings to everyone who steps in from the cold. On this day, family, four-legged friends, and food all come together—a signifier that Christmas has arrived.

The holidays are a cherished and well-thought-out affair for the entire Dabbar clan. From the decor to the dining table, everything is grounded in nostalgia. Family treasures collected over time, handmade stockings, beloved dishware from trips abroad, and vintage hotel silver all find their way into the scheme. Time spent living in Russia is also reflected—art, ornaments, pottery, plates, and glasses are all affectionate reminders of life overseas. To stimulate all of the senses, Susan believes a memorable table needs touches of drama, seduction, romance, and intrigue. "The dinner is about more than just the celebration; it is an opportunity to share your history and family story," she says.

Thick slices of aspen wood chargers are topped with green and ivory Spode Harrogate dinner plates. Rare Wedgwood green frog service dessert dishes, commissioned by Russia's Catherine the Great, also grace the tabletop. Prized porcelain and gold-rimmed glassware gleam and sparkle. Dancing candles, fragrant evergreen, white ranunculus, and whimsical antiques are all part of the vision.

White vintage monogrammed linens are another favorite touch. Exquisite hand-embroidered napkins, marked with the letter D, gently rest under each plate. The napery, a gift from a dear friend, was a previous family heirloom before being passed on to Susan. "I absolutely cherish meaningful touches," she declares. As if to prove her point, a clear glass box filled with homemade cookies, and wrapped in deep green silk ribbon, graces each place setting. The containers serve as clever place cards and delicious parting gifts—just one of the many heartfelt gestures on display.

After dinner everyone retires to the living room for decadent desserts in front of a roaring fire. Coffee is served and gifts are exchanged. For all, it is a good night.

SUGARED CRANBERRIES

Makes 3 ½ cups

These beautiful berries are incredibly simple to make. They are perfect for holiday snacking or for dressing up desserts.

2 cups sugar
One 12-ounce bag cranberries

Combine ½ cup sugar and ½ cup water in a medium saucepan over medium heat. Stir until the sugar is dissolved, 2 to 3 minutes. Mix in the cranberries, stirring until well coated.

Using a slotted spoon, transfer the cranberries to a wire rack; let dry for at least 1 hour.

Working in batches, roll the cranberries in the remaining 1 ½ cups sugar until well coated. Let dry on a wire rack for at least 1 hour before using.

PIMM'S CUP NO. 1

Serves 4

The quintessential British liqueur, Pimm's is a rich amber, gin-based spirit flavored with caramelized oranges and delicate spices. To make a great cocktail, add a selection of fruit and a mixer to a pitcher, then top it off with the liqueur. The possible variations are endless: carbonated lemonade, ginger ale, sparkling wine, Veuve Clicquot, and Fever-Tree Premium Indian tonic water can all stand in for ginger beer, and strawberries can be used with or in place of the oranges.

3 cups crushed ice
2 oranges, cut into half-moon slices
2 Meyer lemons, cut into half-moon slices
1 English cucumber, washed and thinly sliced
2 cups Pimm's liqueur
4 cups ginger beer
5 large mint sprigs
4 small fresh rosemary sprigs

Fill a 32-ounce pitcher with ice. Add a layer of orange slices, followed by a layer of lemon slices, and then cucumber slices. Repeat the layering process until you have used up all of the slices.

Pour in the Pimm's and ginger beer. Mix with a long-handled spoon. Add the mint sprigs and press them down toward the bottom of the pitcher. Divide the drink among four tall glasses and garnish each with a rosemary sprig.

HELP YOURSELF

Guests always welcome the opportunity to relax, mix, mingle, and pace themselves during the holidays. A self-serve bar is perfect for long and festive affairs. Additionally, it frees up the hosts and those preparing the meal. Providing an assortment of beverages along with one easy-to-make signature drink is a thoughtful touch. For Christmas Day, Susan serves a Pimm's Cup No. 1 with oranges and ginger beer—it embodies the taste of the season.

Merry
Christmas

Dinner Menu

Foxhall Road
Washington, D.C.

BEEF TENDERLOIN TEMPERATURE TIPS

Beef tenderloin merits its holiday superstar status. For the best cut of meat, start with high-quality cattle free of antibiotics or added hormones. Tenderloin is an expensive cut that you do not want to overcook. Therefore, a meat thermometer is a must. When cooked correctly, beef tenderloin will melt in your mouth. Mild in flavor, rich and tender, delicious and effortless to make—it is the perfect indulgence for a celebratory occasion.

TEMPERATURE RANGES:
Rare: 120 to 125°F (center is bright red and outside is light red)
Medium rare: 130 to 135°F (center is pink and outside is a light grayish-brown)
Medium: 140 to 145°F (center is pink and outside is brown)
Medium well: 150 to 155°F (center and outside are brown)

HERB-CRUSTED BEEF TENDERLOIN

Serves 8

2 tablespoons chopped rosemary leaves
2 tablespoons chopped flat-leaf parsley leaves
2 tablespoons chopped thyme leaves
2 teaspoons minced garlic
4 pounds center-cut beef tenderloin, trimmed
   and tied with kitchen twine
4 tablespoons unsalted butter, at room temperature
1 tablespoon kosher salt
1 tablespoon freshly ground black and pink pepper

Combine the rosemary, parsley, thyme, and garlic in a small bowl. Place the whole tenderloin on a baking sheet and pat the outside dry with a paper towel. With your hands, spread the butter over both sides of the tenderloin. Then pat with the herb mixture to coat. Season with salt and pepper.

Let the tenderloin sit at room temperature for 45 minutes. This allows the seasonings to penetrate the meat and form a flavorful exterior crust. The resting period also takes the chill off the meat, allowing it to cook more evenly. Meanwhile, preheat the oven to 500°F.

Roast in the preheated oven until the meat reaches your preferred temperature (consult the temperature ranges above). A cooking time of exactly 25 minutes will produce a medium-rare tenderloin. Remove the beef from the oven, cover it tightly with aluminum foil, and allow it to rest at room temperature for 20 minutes.

When ready to serve, remove the twine and cut the tenderloin into ½-inch-thick slices. Transfer the slices to a large serving platter. Pour any accumulated juices from the cutting board over the meat to keep it moist. You can serve it immediately or at room temperature.

Note: As meat cooks, it expands and juices run out, making it difficult to cut a perfectly round fillet. Tying twine around meat helps it keep its shape and holds in the juices. A good butcher can truss the meat for you.

NEW YEAR'S DAY BUFFET
Jan Roden

Falling at the tail end of the holiday season, New Year's Day hardly seems like an ideal time to host a party. Flowers are not at their peak, the weather is dreary and cold, many are tired, and others have overindulged. But do not tell that to Jan Roden. "I am always ready to gather people. Any day of the year. Any excuse. It's my form of recreation."

As soon as the ball drops, Jan slips off to sleep. She is both ready and prepared for her annual celebration with family and dear friends, affectionately dubbed "the inner circle." Opening her quintessential Charlottesville home is her favorite way to ring in the New Year. Armed with make-ahead foods, Jan and her granddaughters set the tables the day before the buffet. "The girls love to help and they will pass anything on a silver tray. It doubles the fun of hosting a party," Jan beams.

After a month of seasonal decor and going all out for the holidays, the hostess elects a clean and neutral palette to mark the occasion. A massive nineteenth-century Carrara marble candy-store-cabinet-cum-buffet embraces clear cut-glass stemware, bottles of Champagne and vodka, and a pitcher of fresh bloody mary mix. An assortment of sparkling waters awaits those who cannot bear booze or bubbly.

A collection of antique ironstone and a few silver serving pieces become the backdrop for customary good-luck fare—black-eyed peas (prosperity), leafy greens (money), pork (progress), fish (abundance), and cornbread (gold). "I love to design menus around my ironware," the collector says. "Having owned the plates and platters for years, it gives me a warm feeling to see them used over and over again. I like knowing that they have been loved for a hundred or more years."

Rather than decorating the tables with fresh flowers, the antiques dealer takes her inspiration from eighteenth- and nineteenth-century tabletops. She opts for fresh citrus with leaves intact, generous bowls of kumquats, and chartreuse fluted beeswax candles in antique candelabras. "For the centerpieces I like to emulate Flemish art, complete with the fruits, nuts, and artifacts. It allows the food to take center stage," she explains.

However, she confesses that her favorite "accessories" are her granddaughters. At ages eleven and twelve, they always come dressed in tutus, soft sweaters, ballet slippers, ribbons, and bows. "They look as if they have just stepped out of a Degas painting." Before the big day, the trio spends weeks making an assortment of confections to send home with their well-fed guests. Little cellophane bags are lavishly filled with irresistible sweets—chocolate, caramel, nuts, and toffees. For many, the New Year's resolutions will have to wait until tomorrow.

COLLECTING IRONSTONE

Ironstone china is a type of vitreous pottery first made in the United Kingdom. It dates to the early nineteenth century. Though typically classified as earthenware, it looks and acts more like stoneware.

The simplicity and functionality of ironstone make it a favorite collectible. Patented by Charles Mason of Stafford-shire, England, this simple tableware was once known as the poor man's porcelain. In the 1840s, undecorated white stoneware was shipped to the colonies. Durable and affordable, ironstone was popular with rural American families and settlers. Many believe that Mason coined the name ironstone to imply that it was strong, hard-wearing china.

Trays and platters are some of the easiest pieces to find and are favorites among collectors for both their functionality and decorative appeal. Tureens with lids, underplates, and ladles are highly coveted. Sets of matching ironstone plates can be hard to find. Luckily, mismatched motifs work beautifully together.

SOUTHERN BLACK-EYED PEAS WITH HAM HOCK

Serves 12

Black-eyed peas are a traditional New Year's Day dish. The peas are believed to bring good luck and prosperity throughout the year. For a full meal, serve with a pan of cornbread and a pot of greens. Collard greens, turnip greens, mustard greens, spinach, kale, and Swiss chard are all excellent options. Serve slices of baguette with this dish so that guests can enjoy every drop.

2 pounds dried black-eyed peas
1 large smoked ham hock
1 large yellow onion, diced
5 cloves garlic, minced
2 tablespoons coarse salt
1 tablespoon cracked black pepper
4 bay leaves
2 cups unsalted vegetable stock

Rinse the beans thoroughly, removing any pebbles or other debris. Add the beans to a large bowl. Add cold water to cover by at least 4 inches. Soak the beans overnight.

The following day, drain the water and rinse the beans. Place the rinsed beans, ham hock, onion, garlic, salt, pepper, and bay leaves in a large stockpot. Add just enough water to cover the beans, then add the vegetable stock.

Bring the beans to a boil. Reduce the heat to a steady simmer. Cook, stirring occasionally, until the beans are tender and the liquid has been absorbed, about 1 hour.

Remove the beans from the heat and discard the bay leaves. Transfer the ham hock to a cutting board. When cool enough to touch, remove the outside skin and the bone. Dice the meat and return it to the pot with the beans. Serve the beans in a tureen with a slotted spoon.

Note: The black-eyed pea, a legume, is a subspecies of the cowpea. Also called a black-eyed bean or goat pea, it is actually a bean.

RESOURCES

ANTIQUES

1stdibs
1stdibs.com

And George
andgeorge.com

Lucullus
lucullusantiques.com

Marché Paul Bert
Serpette
paulbert-serpette.com

Ware M. Porter & Co.
waremporter.com

CANDLES

A. I. Root Company
rootcandles.com

Christian Tortu
christiantortu.fr

Colonial Candle
colonialcandle.com

Creative Candles
creativecandles.com

Diptyque
diptyqueparis.com

Perin-Mowen
perinmowen.com

Thymes
thymes.com

Trudon
trudon.com

CHINA AND DISHWARE

Alberto Pinto
graciousstyle.com

Anna Weatherley
Designs
annaweatherley.com

Bernardaud
bernardaud.com

Canvas Home
canvashomestore.com

Christopher Spitzmiller
christopherspitzmiller
.com

Farmhouse Pottery
farmhousepottery.com

Herend
herendusa.com

India Hicks
indiahicks.com

Mottahedeh
mottahedeh.com

Pickard China
pickardchina.com

Pillivuyt
pillivuytusa.com

Replacements
replacements.com

Rosenthal
rosenthalusa-shop.com

Uriarte Talavera
uriartetalavera.com.mx

Vista Alegre
vistaalegre.com

Wedgwood
wedgwood.com

CRYSTAL AND GLASSWARE

Artland
artland-store.com

Baccarat
baccarat.com

La Rochère
larochere-na.com

Lalique
lalique.com

Lenox
lenox.com

Riedel
riedel.com

Saint-Louis
saint-louis.com

Scully & Scully
scullyandscully.com

Theresienthal
artedona.com

William Yeoward
williamyeowardcrystal
.com

FLATWARE

CB2
cb2.com

Juliska
juliska.com

Michael C. Fina
michaelcfina.com

Sabre Paris
yvonne-estelles.com

Williams Sonoma
williams-sonoma.com

Yamazaki
yamazakitableware.com

GARDEN ACCESSORIES

Mecox Gardens
mecox.com

The Parterre Bench
privatenewport.com

SHOPPE
shoppebham.com

GUEST SOAP

Aésop
aesop.com

Crabtree & Evelyn
crabtree-evelyn.com

Diptyque
diptyqueparis.com

Gilchrist & Soames
gilchristsoames.com

Jo Malone
jomalone.com

Penhaligon's
penhaligons.com

Savon de Marseille
savondemarseille.com

LINENS

Constance Leiter
sharynblondlinens.com

E. Braun & Co.
ebraunnewyork.com

Harmony
harmony-textile.com

Haute Home
hautehome.net

Hibiscus Linens
hibiscuslinens.com

Jacquelyn Reese
jacquelynreese.com

Jenny Johnson Allen
jennyjohnsonallen.com

Julia B.
juliab.com

Juliska
juliska.com

Leontine Linens
leontinelinens.com

Léron
leron.com

Peacock Alley
peacockalley.com

Pioneer Linens
pioneerlinens.com

SFERRA
sferra.com

Society Limonta
societylimonta.com

Walker Valentine
walkervalentine.com

PLACE CARDS AND
INVITATIONS

Alexa Pulitzer
alexapulitzer.com

Connor
connordigital.com

Cotton Paperie
cottonpaperie.com

Crane & Co.
crane.com

Dempsey & Carroll
dempseyandcarroll.com

Mrs. John L. Strong
mrsstrong.com

The Printery
iprintery.com

SILVER

Asprey
asprey.com

Christofle
christofle.com

International
beverlybremer.com

Kirk Stieff
silversuperstore.com

Reed & Barton
reedandbarton.com

Replacements
replacements.com

TABLE ACCESSORIES

Alexandra von
Furstenberg
alexandravon
furstenberg.com

Danielle Rollins
danielledrollins.com

eBay
ebay.com

Etsy
etsy.com

Food52
food52.com

FOUND
foundforthehome.com

FX Dougherty
fxdougherty.com

Get the Gusto
getthegusto.com

One Kings Lane
onekingslane.com

Ralph Lauren Home
ralphlaurenhome.com

Siècle
siecle-paris.com

Tiffany & Co.
tiffany.com

Tom Dixon
tomdixon.net

West Elm
westelm.com

TEXTILES

Brunschwig & Fils
kravet.com

Colefax and Fowler
colefax.com

Cowtan & Tout
cowtan.com

Denise McGaha for
Design Legacy
design-legacy.com

Hines & Company
hinescompany.com

Jasper Fabrics
michaelsmithinc.com

Les Indiennes
lesindiennes.com

Manuel Canovas
manuelcanovas.com

P. Kaufmann
housefabric.com

Raoul Textiles
raoultextiles.com

Ronda Carman
Fine Fabrics
rondacarman.com

Schumacher
fschumacher.com

RECICE INDEX

ACKNOWLEDGMENTS

Abundant thanks and gratitude to everyone featured in this book. I am beyond grateful for your willingness to open your homes and share your thoughts on entertaining. A special thanks to Liz McDermott for your gracious hospitality.

To Matthew Mead, my creative partner in crime, and Michael Hunter for beautifully capturing and immortalizing each person and party showcased within this tome.

To my editor, Sandy Gilbert Freidus, I would like to acknowledge my heartfelt appreciation. I am so lucky to have worked with you on a second book. Thank you for never accepting less than my best efforts and making the whole process enjoyable. You are truly a great friend. To the brilliantly talented book designers Doug Turshen and Steve Turner. Thank you for taking my ideas and making them even better than I could ever have imagined. To everyone at Rizzoli, you are without question the best. A special thank you to publisher Charles Miers, copyeditor Natalie Danford, proofreader Tricia Levi, production manager Maria Pia Gramaglia, and public relations gurus Jessica Napp and Pam Sommers.

Many thanks to the following, who generously provided a few of the pieces featured among the photographs: Haute Home, Juliska, One Kings Lane, and Sferra. Much gratitude goes to Wendy Kvalheim and Paul Wojcik of Mottahedeh and Jim Shreve and Ward Simmons of Baccarat. Meg Fairfax Fielding and Mara Lamb Malcolm, you saved me. Thank you. Your contributions assisted in creating beautiful imagery.

A very special thank you to India Hicks for writing the foreword. I feel so fortunate to know you. I admire that you have forged your own path in life. You inspire me to follow mine.

To Matt, you have been my rock through every phase of this project. You are more than just a partner; you are my best friend. Thank you for your love, kindness, and support. You make me smile every day. Mason, each day I look forward to your texts, photos, and recipes. I am so proud of you. Here is to the next chapter. Jack and Michael, I am so happy to have you both in my life. Thank you for your love and cheer. Much love to my family for your enthusiasm. I am so fortunate that I was encouraged as a child to dream big. Thank you to my mom and dad for always telling me, "If you can dream it, you can become it." Michelle, Marilyn, and Tiffany, you are great sisters. Profuse gratitude goes to Tiffany, who generously responded to my many out-of-the-blue requests for feedback. Much love and many thanks to my wonderful in-laws, Dinah and David Whitaker, for always taking an interest in my book.

To my wonderful friends who have encouraged my many endeavors—you know who you are and how much I adore you. I am blessed to have so many amazing people in my life. I can only beg forgiveness of those who have supported me over the years and whose names I have failed to mention.

First published in the United States of America in 2019 by
Rizzoli International Publications, Inc.
300 Park Avenue South
New York, NY 10010
www.rizzoliusa.com

Copyright © 2019 Ronda Carman
Principal photography: Matthew Mead and Michael Hunter

Publisher: Charles Miers
Editor: Sandra Gilbert Freidus
Design: Doug Turshen and Steve Turner
Production Manager: Colin Hough Trapp
Managing Editor: Lynn Scrabis

Printed in China

2019 2020 2021 2022 / 10 9 8 7 6 5 4 3 2 1

ISBN: 978-0-8478-6601-4
Library of Congress Control Number: 2019937993

Visit us online:
Facebook.com/RizzoliNewYork
Twitter: @Rizzoli_Books
Instagram.com/RizzoliBooks
Pinterest.com/RizzoliBooks
Youtube.com/user/RizzoliNY
Issuu.com/Rizzoli